BEYOND WORDS

Prentice-Hall Speech Communication Series

Larry L. Barker
Robert J. Kibler
Consulting Editors

BEYOND WORDS

an introduction to nonverbal communication

RANDALL P. HARRISON

Department of Communication
Michigan State University

Prentice-Hall, Inc., *Englewood Cliffs, New Jersey*

Library of Congress Cataloging in Publication Data

HARRISON, RANDALL P.
    Beyond Words.

    (Prentice-Hall series in speech communication)
    Bibliography: p.
    1. Nonverbal communication.   I. Title.
BF637.C45H34   153   73–17202
ISBN 0–13–076141–9
ISBN 0–13–076133–8 (pbk.)

© 1974 by Prentice-Hall, Inc.,
Englewood Cliffs, New Jersey

Prentice-Hall International, Inc., London
Prentice-Hall of Australia, Pty. Ltd., Sydney
Prentice-Hall of Canada, Ltd., Toronto
Prentice-Hall of India Private Limited, New Delhi
Prentice-Hall of Japan, Inc., Tokyo

contents

PART IV
CONCLUSION

APPENDIXES

to the reader

This book is about *nonverbal* communication.

The field of nonverbal communication is exciting, fast-moving, multi-faceted, rapidly growing. It provides all the challenge of a good intellectual puzzle. Yet it also promises practical applications in your daily life. It has implications for you as a communicator—and as a human being.

Recently, a number of books have touched on nonverbal communication. Some are popular and easy to read. Some are erudite and profound. But most focus on one aspect of nonverbal communication only. Many miss the sweep of nonverbal communication as it is understood today.

This book is designed as an introduction, a key for unlocking the reservoir of recent findings. It should serve as a useful map to the nonverbal domain, alerting you to interesting areas, helping you through unfamiliar terrain.

The book lays a foundation on which to build further understanding. It provides a conceptual framework, including the growing vocabulary used by researchers and practitioners. In its organization and selection of examples, the book is designed to challenge and stimulate your thinking. It will sharpen the intellectual tools you will use in your own explorations, in other readings, in the field, in your personal life.

I hope you enjoy the book—and profit from it.

acknowledgment

To . . .

Michael Argyle
Larry Barker
John Bjørn Bear
David Berlo
Erwin Bettinghaus
Ray L. Birdwhistell
Jerry Boucher
Leonard Breger
Beckie Brenneman
Walter Brovald
Dena Brunstig
Richard Budd
James H. Campbell
Walter Coblenz
Akiba Cohen
Wayne Crouch
Don Cushman
Charles Darwin
Joel Davitz
Joe DeRivera
Joseph Dermer
Allen Dittmann
Albert Einstein
Paul Ekman
Phoebe Ellsworth
Arthur Elstein
Ralph Exline
John R. Farley
John Frahm
Dan Freedman

Sigmund Freud
Wallace V. Friesen
Doug Fuchs
B. K. L. Genova
Erving Goffman
Bradley Greenberg
Gretchen Grover
Louis Guttman
Edward T. Hall
Ann Halsted
George Halsted
Jane Halsted
Marian Halsted
Rex Harrison
Zan Harrison
Hal W. Hepler
Herblock
Henry Hetland
Dorothy Hoover
M. Lance Hooper
Gerald D. Hursh
Eugene Jacobson
Hillary Jason
John Johnson
Sidney Jourard
Natan Katzman
Mark Knapp
Klaus Krippendorff
Hideya Kumata
James Lamb

Marilyn Legge
Joanne Leonard
Colby Lewis
Harriett Lukes
Nathan Maccoby
Malcolm S. MacLean, Jr.
Edward Malmstrom
Marcel Marceau
Miles Martin
Ed McCoy
Albert Mehrabian
Gerald R. Miller
Marty Miller
Clyde Morris
Sharon Nelton
Charles Osgood
Bill Paisley
Ed Parker
David Pascal
Dorothea Paul
Joseph Paul
Ithiel de Sola Pool
Jeremy Pool
Edna Day Powers
Arthur Rittenberg
Everett M. Rogers
Milton Rokeach
Howard M. Rosenfeld
Richard Rudner
Jurgen Ruesch

Albert Scheflen
Wilbur Schramm
Charles Schuller
Thomas Sebeok
Doug Solomon
Mark Steinberg
Paul Stimson
Albert Talbott
Percy Tannenbaum
Lee Thayer
Arnie T. Thompson
Catherine Paul Thompson
Dozier Thornton
Sylvan Tomkins
Pete Troldahl
John Useem
Kensile Van Holde
Fred Waisanen
Barb Walker
Michael Watson
Ted Weber
Arthur Weld
George Wheeler
Ray Wiman
Joe Woelfel
Sol Worth
Frank Lloyd Wright
Karen Zekus
Carl Zlatchin

... *THANKS*,
r. p. h.

INTRODUCTION

1

nonverbal cues

LEARNING TIPS

This chapter is designed to

1. Stimulate your *thinking* about nonverbal communication.

2. Sensitize you to different *types* of nonverbal cues.

3. Encourage you to examine the *inferences* you make on the basis of nonverbal cues.

4. Draw your attention to the *differences* between verbal and nonverbal symbols.

5. Engage your thinking about the possible *relationships* between verbal and nonverbal messages.

THOUGHT STARTERS

1. What nonverbal cues do you use *most* in communication?

2. How accurate are you in *interpreting* nonverbal cues?

3. What *proportion* of your communication is nonverbal as opposed to verbal?

FIGURE 1-1 Instructions for "Right"–"Right" Cartoon.

STOP!

before turning the page
read the instructions below

ON THE FOLLOWING PAGE . . .

. . . is a verbal-nonverbal message designed to increase your sensitivity to nonverbal cues. To ensure maximum learning, please follow these instructions carefully:

1. Take an opaque piece of paper. (A 5- by 8-inch file card is fine.)

2. Slip it between the next two pages, being careful not to look at the picture on the left-hand page. (See Figure 1-1A.)

3. Turn the page so that the paper completely covers the left page. (See Figure 1-1B.)

4. Slowly slide the paper down to reveal the number "1" in each margin. (See Figure 1-1C.)

5. Answer the overall questions: What do you know now? How do you know that? Then answer questions 1a, 1b, and 1c.

6. Slide the paper down to reveal number 2; answer the general questions again and then the specific questions related to 2.

7. Continue this procedure to the bottom of the page.

Figure 1-2 The Nonverbal Sensitivity Test.

THE QUESTIONS BELOW ARE KEYED TO FIGURE 1-2. For complete instructions, turn back one page.

Part I

1. What do you know now about the message in the figure? How do you know that?
   a. Both words are being spoken rather than thought.   T F
   b. The "RIGHT" on the left is being said loudest.   T F
   c. "Right" here means
      __(1) Correct; __(2) A political leaning; __(3) Starboard; __(4) A just claim; __(5) It's impossible to say.
2. What do you know now? How do you know that?
   a. The individual on the left is under 30.   T F
   b. The individual on the right is a female.   T F
   c. This is going to be
      __(1) Two soldiers marching; __(2) A policeman giving instructions to a motorist; __(3) Two motorcyclists making a turn; __(4) A conversation; __(5) A political rally.
3. What do you know now? How?
   a. The individual on the left is
      __(1) Happy; __(2) Surprised; __(3) Disgusted; __(4) Angry; (5) Sad.
   b. The individual on the right is
      __(1) Surprised; __(2) Happy; __(3) Alert; __(4) Sad; __(5) Angry.
   c. The individual on the right is under 30.   T F

4. What do you know now? How?
   a. The individual on the left is
      __(1) Happy; __(2) Angry; __(3) Fiendish; __(4) Sad;
      __(5) Sleepy.
   b. The man on the right is
      __(1) Dumb; __(2) Bright; __(3) Happy; __(4) 1 and 3;
      __(5) 2 and 3.
   c. The verbal expressions seem to agree with the pictures.   T   F
5. What do you know now? How?
   a. The individual on the left is
      __(1) Well-to-do; __(2) Dominant; __(3) Over 35; __(4)
      All of these; __(5) None of these.
   b. The individual on the right is
      __(1) A policeman; __(2) A bellhop; __(3) A fireman;
      __(4) A student; __(5) None of these.
   c. The scene is aboard ship.
      __(1) True; __(2) False; __(3) Maybe.
6. What do you know now? How?
   a. The man on the left is
      __(1) In agreement; __(2) In mourning; __(3) Incorrigi-
      ble; __(4) All of these; __(5) None of these.
   b. The man on the right is
      __(1) In disagreement; __(2) In mourning; __(3) Intelli-
      gent; __(4) All of these; __(5) None of these.
   c. The man on the right is a snappy dresser.   T   F
7. What do you know now? How?
   a. The man on the left is
      __(1) Trustworthy; __(2) Honest; __(3) Hopeful; __(4)
      A sneak; __(5) None of these.
   b. The man on the right is
      __(1) Married; __(2) A Mason; __(3) Forgetful; __(4)
      All of these; __(5) None of these.
   c. The sign on the right is
      __(1) A stop sign; __(2) A RR Crossing sign; __(3) A
      tavern sign; __(4) An astrological sign; __(5) None of these.
8. What do you know now? How?
   a. The man in the background is
      __(1) A bellhop; __(2) A policeman; __(3) A fireman;
      __(4) A student; __(5) None of these.
   b. The star on the car is the Star of David.   T   F
   c. The light on the vehicle means it's a Good Humor wagon.   T   F
   d. The object to the right is
      __(1) A still; __(2) A machine for generating Indian smoke

signals; ___(3) A Good Humor wagon; ___(4) A space vehicle; ___(5) None of these.

9. What do you know now? How?
   a. The briefcase to the left has the symbol of
      ___(1) The U.S. Treasury; ___(2) The Internal Revenue Service; ___(3) The Justice Department; ___(4) The Toledo Scales Corporation; ___(5) None of the above.
   b. The suitcase to the right has the symbol(s) of
      ___(1) American Airlines; ___(2) Pan Am; ___(3) *Playboy*; ___(4) All of these; ___(5) None of these.
   c. The time on the clock suggests
      ___(1) This is a social meeting; ___(2) This is a business meeting; ___(3) It's time for a real blast; ___(4) All of these; ___(5) None of these.
   d. The man on the left is
      ___(1) Competent; ___(2) Untrustworthy; ___(3) Dynamic; ___(4) All of these; ___(5) None of these.
   e. The man on the right is
      ___(1) Competent; ___(2) Trustworthy; ___(3) Dynamic; ___(4) All of these; ___(5) None of these.

Part II Summary

1. What can you infer about the individuals from their (a) Postures? (b) Use of space? (c) Apparel? (d) Expressions? (e) Body types? (f) Gestures? (g) Possessions?
2. What specific cues are you using to make these inferences?
3. Final thought: Is violence (or the threat of violence) nonverbal communication?

For the most frequent answers to the questions in Part I, see Appendix A.

NONVERBAL CUE ANALYSIS

You have just seen the world's first space-jacking attempt!

(At least you are supposed to have just seen it. If you haven't, go back and work the exercise.)

(If you still haven't seen it, you are a very untrustworthy type. You probably also read the ends of mysteries first. Check with your instructor and he will assign you a less-interesting text.)

Individuals who discuss this picture are often struck with:

- *The sheer wealth of nonverbal cues.* Even in a simple cartoon such as this we find hundreds of nonverbal cues.
- *The way even minor cues elicit distinct meanings.* For example, just seeing the eyebrows tilt up or down elicits a strong impression of each man.
- *The complexity of our inference processes.* We seem to say to ourselves: "That cue must mean . . . and combined with that cue it must mean . . . but this other cue countermands that, so it must really mean . . . ," and so on.
- *Our low awareness level.* We apparently perceive and process nonverbal cues, often with little awareness that we have taken them in, that we have responded to them, that they are influencing our behavior.
- *The differing interpretations made by individuals.* For example, most people see the handshake as a sign of agreement, but that is not true in all cultures; meanwhile, some people see the crossed fingers as "hoping" while others interpret it as "deception."
- *The complex relationship between verbal and nonverbal symbols.* We try to make them fit together; and when they don't we reexamine again and again.

What other points struck you?

Some of the subtler points made about this experience include the following:

1. Strictly from seeing a single word in isolation—for example, "right"—it's hard to be certain of its intended meaning.
2. Punctuation marks—or in speech, inflection and tone of voice—are important in understanding a verbal message. (Try these alternative punctuations for the "Right"–"Right" cartoon: (a) Right? Right! (b) Right. Right! (c) Right! Right?)
3. Although the words seem ambiguous at first, the nonverbal context reduces uncertainty about what might be meant. ("Right" has literally dozens of possible meanings; these are reduced to a few probable meanings when nonverbal cues are taken into account.)
4. Type size and style seem to be kinds of "nonverbal" cues. (Why, for example, should largeness and boldness be equated with loudness?)
5. The comic-strip speech balloon and thought balloon are other nonverbal cues that children in our culture learn at an early age.
6. When there is a disagreement between the verbal message and the nonverbal message we tend to believe the nonverbal message.
7. This cartoon itself is a special kind of nonverbal communication; it allows for certain nonverbal cues to be exaggerated while other normal cues are dropped out.
8. Facial appearance and expression tell us much—but a surprising amount of information also comes from clothing, possessions, and body posture.

9. Many nonverbal signs, such as those identifying a police car, can be recognized quickly even at great distances.

10. Our ability to decode some nonverbal signs stems from our previous experience; for instance, college-aged individuals may be more familiar with the *Playboy* bunny logo than with the symbol of the Internal Revenue Service, and males may be more alert to the bunny than females.

Do you agree with these points? Why? Why not?

NONVERBAL CUES IN COMMUNICATION

The "Right"–"Right" cartoon provides us with an initial glimpse of the nonverbal world. Perhaps before you began this book, the term "communication" conjured up—primarily—an image of words. Words tripping off the tongue. Words flowing from the pen. Words cascading on the ear. Printed words tugging at the eye. But as the "Right"–"Right" cartoon suggests, human communication includes much more than words.

Let's take a typical American middle-class male as he moves through a day's activities. What are the nonverbal cues he might produce—and process?

He begins each day by preparing himself as a nonverbal message to the world. He shaves his face. Or at least part of it, having recently grown sideburns and a mustache to appear younger and more debonair. He uses toothpaste, soap, and deodorant to manage his messages of smell. He adds cologne, after-shave lotion, or perfume. He brushes his hair into a style that is current—or at least relatively acceptable to those he meets. Some of his friends, of course, don wigs, to look more youthful or more stylish. And both his male and female friends use an array of cosmetics, to enhance their best features, to cover blemishes, to accent the features currently in fad.

Our American male dresses not only to protect his tender hide from the elements; his clothes are a statement about himself. He matches his garb to the events of the day: play, work; informal, formal; important, unimportant. His dress reflects the way he feels about himself, the way he feels generally: happy, sad; youthful, mature; fashionable, conservative. Again, his clothing may accent his best features—or remold those that are not so great. He may wear padded shoulders, just as his wife may wear a padded bra. Both he and she may squeeze into "foundation garments" to smooth the bulging tummy, to slim the too-plump hips.

The costume may be topped off with a display of jewelry. Wedding ring. Class ring or fraternal ring. Lapel buttons. A tie-clasp with a business trademark. He would love to shock his colleagues by showing up in love beads, peace signs, and ankh symbol. But so far he has stifled such urges. He realizes all too well that jewelry can be used to display wealth, or taste, or political leaning, or definition of the situation.

While our typical male completes his adornments, he may be listening to music or watching television. Breakfast may be announced by the smell of bacon or the aroma of coffee. At the breakfast table, he selects his food from colorful packages. He reads the facial expression of his spouse—and decides whether to converse or read the morning comics. He savors his food, wondering whether to compliment or complain. Breakfast over, he gives his wife a passionate farewell kiss and starts out the door. Noting the black ominous clouds, he returns for an umbrella. And another kiss.

On the way to work, he literally bets his life on nonverbal communication. Every time he steps off the curb or into an automobile, he wagers that others will know the nonverbal codes he does. He counts on others to have the same meanings for yellow lines painted down the middle of the road. For red and green lights. For diamond-shaped or triangular-shaped signs. For the policeman's gesture. For the ambulance's flashing red light. For the driver's turn signal.

At the office, he interacts with friends and associates. He shakes hands in meeting or agreement. He nods to friends and waves to acquaintances. He flashes approval with a smile. Or he telegraphs disapproval with a frown. As he verbalizes, he also "talks with his hands." He regulates his interactions with a complex pattern of eye contact, head nods, body movement. He decodes the nonverbal messages of others: their status, their like or dislike, their willingness to communicate.

He arranges his own office to reflect his status and his personal taste. He rearranges it to facilitate interaction. Or to encourage its termination. He allots time: to significant activities and to insignificant activities, to important people and to less important people. He makes presentations, perhaps with the aid of charts, slides, film, videotape. He receives information, pictorially, graphically, color-coded, sized for importance.

Out to lunch, he chooses a restaurant on the basis of its appearance. The decor suggests a type of food: Swiss, Chinese, French, Italian. Its appearance also suggests how expensive the meal will be, and whether the establishment will be clean enough for him. Strolling after lunch, his eye is caught by signs, ads, window displays. He purchases an item that has been carefully designed to suggest durability, efficiency, and modernity. Along the street, he shakes his head at the street people, the dress and behavior of others from other lands, other classes, other races.

Back at work, he runs meetings and participates in others, constantly picking up nonverbal cues of agreement, disagreement, tension, relaxation, confusion, confidence. He meets salesmen and instantly makes judgments about their competency and honesty. He makes persuasive attempts himself, carefully engineering his presentation of self to "put his best foot forward."

The workday done, he returns home, pleased (or displeased) with what his domicile says about his station in life. He notes the order (or disorder) of the living room. He tries to detect from odors what he will have for dinner. And he concludes, in the words of the old ad slogan, "Nothin' says lovin' like somethin' from the oven." He hugs his wife and then relaxes with hi-fi or television. Even out of the room, he knows from the theme music when his favorite program is about to start. He sees an awesome array of ads, packages and products, trademarks and logos, pictures and pitches. On the news, he sees images from around the world or from as far away as the moon. When the drama starts, he knows the good guys because they wear white hats. He knows from the background music when to feel tension and suspense. He sits there, picking programs, products—and perhaps presidents—on the basis of nonverbal cues.

If it's a special night, he may take his wife to a movie, or a concert, or the ballet. Or he may indulge one of his hobbies: photography, painting, playing a musical instrument. Or he may flip through his supply of colorful magazines or the temptingly illustrated catalogs or the brochures with scenic, far-off vacation spots.

His wife comes in, wearing his favorite perfume. She gives him a seductive look and he scurries off to bed. Cuddled close, he scratches her back tenderly and she purrs, contentedly. But after a few minutes, his hand stops moving.

She nudges him to see if he's asleep. Silence.

Then she says softly, "Aren't you even going to kiss me good night?"

And he answers with an eloquent nonverbal snore.

Through the day, modern man goes about his problem solving. He uses nonverbal cues to reduce uncertainty. Other cues increase uncertainty. And he explores further. He relies on communication to identify problems. To articulate his own needs. To learn the needs of others. He counts on communication to alert him to alternatives. He uses communication to negotiate solutions. He gives commands. He takes orders. He processes news. He makes his decision. He communicates his vote. He uses communication for relaxation and refreshment. And throughout this constant flow of communication runs an important stream of nonverbal cues.

FURTHER EXERCISES IN NONVERBAL SENSITIVITY

The following exercises are designed to increase your awareness of nonverbal stimuli and your own decoding processes. In each exercise try to (a) identify the specific nonverbal stimuli or cues, (b) specify the interpretation you have for those cues, and (c) determine how you came to that meaning or interpretation.

1. Close your eyes for a minute or more and experience all your senses as fully as you can. Then open your eyes and answer the following:
   a. What did you hear?
   b. What did you smell?
   c. What did you feel with your skin? (Temperatures? Pressures?)
   d. What did you taste?
   e. What did you experience of your inner body (e.g., muscle tensions, stomach contractions, breathing)?

2. Take a piece of fabric. With your eyes closed, rub it between your fingers, on the back of your hand, on your cheek. Then try it with a different piece of fabric. What distinguishes them? Could you tell them apart without looking at them? How aware are you of your clothing, the way different fabrics feel against your body?

3. Take (a) a soda cracker, (b) a square of chocolate, and (c) something sour such as an olive or a pickle. Break the soda cracker in half and lick the salt off the cracker. Then place the cracker on the roof of your mouth and let it melt. Next take the square of chocolate. Smell it. Lick it. Then place it on the roof of your mouth and let it melt. Next take the olive (or pickle). Sniff it. Lick it. Suck on it. Eat It. Finally, take the other half of your soda cracker. Eat it aggressively, so it really crunches between your teeth. What did you learn about the way you experience food?

4. Take a seat in a public place, such as a coffee shop or a restaurant, and observe the people as they come in. What can you tell about them from their body posture and movements? Facial features and expressions? Clothing and personal articles?

5. In a similar setting, observe the interaction between people. Strictly from body posture, gestures, and facial expressions, what can you infer about the relationships?

6. Repeat the last two exercises in different settings, where you can get a varied range of people to observe (e.g., try a bus station, a downtown hotel, a shopping center, a zoo, a movie house, a sporting event).

7. Watch three different television segments with the sound turned off. What messages are transmitted nonverbally? How much of what is going on can you understand just watching the video? Do the three segments differ in the amount and type of nonverbal cues used?

8. Find a newsstand with a large selection of magazines. Stand back and try to determine—without reading any of the verbal messages—the

audience for each magazine. How do the magazines differ? What nonverbal cues are used to attract potential readers?

9. Analyze trademarks in ads, labels, and packaging. What distinguishes modern trademarks? What makes for a good trademark? Do some colors and shapes seem to have distinct associations (e.g., pleasant or unpleasant, strong or weak, active or passive, masculine or feminine)?

10. Watch a late-evening TV talk show or a Sunday afternoon interview program. Without the sound, what impressions can you derive from nonverbal cues? What can you tell about the individuals? Their interpersonal relationships?

GROUP DISCUSSION POSSIBILITIES

The following questions may be particularly useful in group discussion to summarize the experiences of this chapter.

1. How many different types of nonverbal cues can you identify?

2. On the basis of the "Right"–"Right" cartoon and daily experience, what seems to be the relationship between verbal messages and nonverbal messages?

3. On the basis of the cartoon and your experiences in life, how important do you think nonverbal cues are?

FURTHER READINGS

Bosmajian, Haig A. (ed.) *The Rhetoric of Nonverbal Communication.* Glenview, Ill.: Scott, Foresman, 1971.

Gunther, Bernard. *Sense Relaxation.* New York: Macmillan, 1968.

Ruesch, Jurgen, and Weldon Kees. *Nonverbal Communication: Notes on the Visual Perception of Human Relations.* Berkeley: University of California Press, 1956; 2nd ed., 1971.

2

nonverbal
communication

This chapter is designed to

1. Provide you with a preliminary definition of nonverbal communication.

2. Introduce you to alternative ways of mapping or defining the nonverbal domain.

3. Alert you to:
   - two basic problems in nonverbal communication:

     the problem of "missed cues"—not catching available nonverbal signs; and

     the problem of "miscues"—catching but misinterpreting nonverbal events.

   - two fundamental miscues, or types of error:

     assigning meaning to meaningless events; and
     not assigning meanings to meaningful events.

   - two levels of meaning confusion:

     knowing what the sign denotes or refers to; and
     knowing what the sign connotes—what feelings and associations it elicits.

4. Introduce you to:
   - these key terms:

cue	*information*
nonverbal communication	*exchange*
sign	

- these additional concepts:

sign language

action language

object language

kinesics

informative behavior

interactive behavior

communicative behavior

immediacy dimension

power dimension

responsiveness dimension

THOUGHT STARTERS

1. Are all nonverbal *cues* nonverbal *communication?*

2. Is the Red Cross symbol used in all countries of the world?

3. If you met an Intelligence from outer space, how would you communicate with him (or her, or it)?

You are sitting alone in your study one evening watching the stars when suddenly one seems to grow in intensity and advance toward you. Quickly the room is filled with an intense white light. And then, in a twinkling, you are no longer in your study. You are in a long white corridor.

Speedily reviewing your recent ingestions you conclude that you should be relatively sober. The most logical explanation is that you have been whisked away by some Visiting Intelligence from outer space. You begin to walk down the corridor, your senses somewhat sharpened by the novelty of your situation. The floor appears to be tilted, but you soon become accustomed to walking on the diagonal. As you round a bend in the corridor you notice a mark on the wall. It looks like this: +. It is about 3 inches high, a fairly thin black line against the all-white surface.

What do you make of the mark?

LET'S PAUSE IN THIS FASCINATING ADVENTURE to analyze the problems you could have.

Missed Cues

First of all, you could have missed seeing the mark altogether. This is not uncommon in our daily rounds. In the flood of cues that flow past our senses, it is easy to miss important events. Most of us have had the experience of missing our exit on a freeway or failing to take the right turnoff on a journey. Most of us have gone to plays or movies and later discovered that we caught some cues that others missed—and perhaps missed some that they caught. When reading mysteries, we thread our way through a host of cues. And when we're done, if the author has been

it was a traffic sign—of some sort. We didn't miss the sign. But neither of us had the slightest idea what it meant. The sign, of course, was the international symbol for "yield," which is now diffusing throughout the United States. Fortunately for us, we were not wiped out by some unyielding South African.

Similar levels of recognition exist in interpersonal interaction. Consider this situation: you and Best Friend of the Opposite Sex are at a dinner party with Important Others. During the conversation, BFOS begins to talk about a subject which you feel is very sensitive. BFOS is nudged under the table. BFOS continues . . . and is nudged still harder. Suddenly, BFOS stops and says: "Why are you kicking me under the table?" What was a missed cue has just penetrated BFOS's consciousness to become a signal, but one without meaning. Meanwhile, others at the table may make an immediate interpretation. And you may be demoting former BF to FB (for Foul Ball)—or some other appropriate set of initials.

PROBLEMS IN MEANING

You advance and inspect the "+" mark more closely. It does not appear to be a mere crack in the wall. You rule out a random event such as an intergalactic earthquake. The mark appears to have been applied to the white wall with some black substance. You conclude that perhaps it is a mark which, for some being, has meaning. But now the question is: How do you know what it means?

As with verbal symbols, nonverbal cues can elicit meanings at two levels. In trying to communicate with another person it is possible to "go wrong" at either level.

Denotation

The first level is what is known as *denotative* meaning. Symbols *denote*, or refer to, things other than themselves. They indicate objects, events, and concepts. The word "cross" denotes a particular type of configuration—the joining of a vertical and a horizontal line—things which have this general shape: +. But the word "cross" can also be used to denote other things, for example, a state of mind: "He sure is *cross* today."

An initial possibility of meaning confusion thus arises at the denotative level. When using a symbol we have to decide which of its possible denotations is indicated. Does "cross" refer to a configuration of two lines, or to someone's mental state? Does "right" refer to a direction, or a political stance? Let's take a nonverbal example.

At an international conference, I sat next to a gentleman from Thailand. We had just changed meeting rooms and another gentleman, from an African nation, looked in the doorway to see if that was the right place. The Thai beckoned for the man to come in. But the African merely waved and went on. The Thai jumped up and went after the man. What happened?

In the United States and many other parts of the world we beckon to someone with our palm up. We may waggle just the index finger or all our fingers. But the gesture denotes: "Come here." In Thailand, however, the "come here" gesture is delivered with the palm down, all the fingers moving, and the hand held at head level. My friend from Thailand had traveled in international circles long enough to realize that his "come here" gesture had not denoted "come here" to the African. It had been misinterpreted instead as merely a friendly wave. Even when people share denotative meanings, however, there is a second level of meaning confusion.

Connotation

Symbols, as we use them, do more than point to objects or events in the outside world. For the user, they usually elicit a whole host of associations, feelings—*connotations*. This is the *connotative* level of meaning. And sometimes, symbols have very powerful connotations; they elicit very strong feelings.

You might, for example, decide that "cross" does denote—refer to—the configuration that looks like this: +. But now, if you are a devout Christian, that symbol may be particularly meaningful to you. You will see it as powerful, positive, strong. Men have died in the sign of the cross. On the other hand, if you are not a religious person, you may be somewhat indifferent to the cross. If you belong to a non-Christian religion, you may feel hostile toward the cross. And if you were a thief in ancient Jerusalem, you would probably have associated the cross with punishment and death, hardly a positive reaction.

To return to the example of nonverbal beckoning gestures, many cultures of the world use the same motion that we use to denote "come here." But beckoning with the index finger is reserved in many societies for calling children or servants. If you so signaled an equal or a superior, he would understand what you wanted, what your gesture was meant to denote. But the gesture would be taken as a grave insult. It would elicit strong negative feelings. He might refuse to come, even though he understood what you wanted. Or if he did come, you might have great difficulty communicating; you did not share connotative meanings for what to him was an important symbol.

Thus, whenever humans interact using symbols, they may have a mismatch of meanings at two levels. They may be using the same symbol to denote two different things. But even if they share denotative meanings, they may diverge at the connotative level. For one individual, the symbol may elicit good, strong, active feelings. For another individual, the same symbol may elicit feelings which are bad, weak, and passive.

> As you look at the "+" on the wall, all this knowledge runs through your mind. (After all, you have nothing else to do in that blank white corridor. And it's as good a time as any to review your coursework . . . in case you do get back to Earth.)
>
> You decide that if you were on Earth the "+" mark might denote the cross, which in turn might signify Christianity. Or the mark might denote a "plus sign," which in turn might indicate "addition," or "mathematics generally," or "a positive value." At the connotative level, these denotations may be eliciting a range of feelings. You may, first of all, feel reassured that these unseen creatures use symbols similar to ones we know on Earth. If you are a Christian, you may feel very pleased. On the other hand, if your faith is Islam, you may be feeling: "Great Allah! I've been delivered into the hands of the Infidel!" Similarly, if you are a mathematician, you may be delighted. But if you hate mathematics, you may be dismayed. Perhaps these folks speak nothing but algebra.
>
> You touch the mark. And nothing happens. So you walk on, rounding another bend, and suddenly you are confronted with a sliding door. On it is another "+" somewhat larger and bolder. You are now convinced this is some kind of meaningful sign. You cannot get the door open and it does not open for you. You do note what appears to be a bench, so you sit down and wait. At this point, you realize that in your study you were holding this book in your hand and it is still with you. So, pondering the mysterious "+," you review Figure 2-1.

DEFINING NONVERBAL COMMUNICATION

In Chapter 1 we talked very generally about nonverbal cues, without ever defining precisely what we meant by "cue." In this chapter we have begun to use other terms, such as nonverbal communication, sign, symbol,

FIGURE 2-1   Decoding Decision Tree.

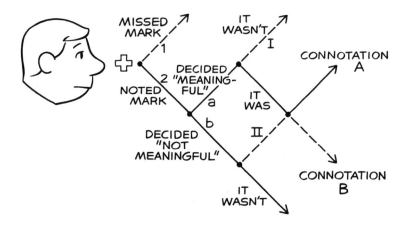

Our decoder passed a mark: +. He may miss it (1) or note it (2). If he notes it, he may decide: (a) it is "meaningful"; or (b) it is "not meaningful." I illustrates one type of error: where the decoder thought the mark was meaningful—but it wasn't. II illustrates a second kind of error: the decoder decided "not meaningful"—but it was. Even if the decoder decides it was meaningful, and is right, he still may have to choose between different connotations, e.g., A or B.

signal. It is now time to shift gears and begin to be more precise about our denotations for key terms. We need to hone our perceptions and sharpen our intellectual tools for the hard work ahead.

A *cue*, as we have used the term, refers very broadly to any stimulus (a) that is above the sensory threshold of some human being and (b) for which that human has some response. *Nonverbal cues* are all those stimuli we respond to—other than the spoken or written word. In this chapter we have begun to distinguish among different kinds of cues. And we will now want to distinguish between the broad category of *nonverbal cues* and the more specific process of *nonverbal communication*.

The term "nonverbal communication" has been applied to a bewildering array of events. Everything from the territoriality of animals to the protocol of diplomats. From facial expressions to muscle twitches. From inner, but inexpressible, feelings to outdoor, public monuments. From the message of massage to the persuasion of a punch. From dance and drama to music and mime. From the flow of affect to the flow of traffic. From extrasensory perception to the economic policies of international power blocks. From fashion and fad to architecture and analog computer. From the smell of roses to the taste of steak. From Freudian symbol to astrological sign. From the rhetoric of violence to the rhetoric of topless dancers.[1]

This is a fascinating spectrum. But it is also a rather confusing hodge-podge when we are first trying to get our bearings. As a jumping-off point, we will deal with nonverbal communication as follows:

Nonverbal communication is the exchange of information through nonlinguistic signs. This proposition, in turn, contains some key terms which need elaboration:

- *Sign:* a sign is a stimulus which, for some communicator, "stands for" something else; it "means" something above and beyond itself.
- *Nonlinguistic:* the primary linguistic sign is the word in spoken or written form; thus we are concerned with the full range of nonword signs.
- *Information:* in a technical sense, information involves the manipulation of uncertainty; it suggests that, for some organism, uncertainty is decreased —or increased.
- *Exchange:* by exchange we mean to imply more than one communicator linked in some way so that at least one of them can respond to the signs produced by the other. The easiest example is two individuals in face-to-face interaction. But we would include mass-media systems, where one communicator encodes messages, in one time and place, for other communicators at another time and place. We would even include such communicators as Rembrandt and da Vinci—long dead, but whose messages still find an audience.

Let's see what this definition looks like in a less verbal diagram:

$$A \rightleftarrows M \rightleftarrows B$$

We'll call our first communicator "A" (a very original system of labeling). And our second communicator will be (you guessed it) "B." The "M"? (You're way ahead of me). That stands for "message." Now we will add one other element:

$$\left\{I\updownarrow\right\}A \rightleftarrows M \rightleftarrows B\left\{I\updownarrow\right\}$$

The "I" in the thought balloon stands for "information." We're suggesting that, through the exchange of messages, information level (or uncertainty) rises and falls.

[1] See, for example, Haig A. Bosmajian (ed.), *The Rhetoric of Nonverbal Communication* (Glenview, Ill.: Scott, Foresman, 1971), pp. 98–105.

Finally, our definition proposes that messages are made up of signs: verbal signs (Sv), nonverbal signs (Snv), or both (Sv.nv).

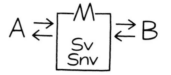

In focusing on nonverbal communication, our interest is in the non-linguistic signs; but we realize that in any communication situation the linguistic and nonlinguistic signs may interweave and influence each other.

I think the definition we have proposed is a useful way to approach nonverbal communication. Unfortunately, not all communication scholars and practitioners agree. Many (in fact, if I must be honest, *most*) take somewhat divergent views. If you are only going to read this book, this definition is all you'll ever need. If, however, you think you'll ever be tempted to read other books on communication or nonverbal communication, then perhaps you'd better know about the alternative approaches.

ALTERNATIVE MAPPINGS OF THE NONVERBAL DOMAIN

Providing a useful definition is a little like drawing a map. You can present a map that includes just one city . . . or the whole Western Hemisphere. You can present a map that has a great amount of detail or one with bare outlines. And you can present a map that emphasizes different *kinds* of detail. You can draw a political map (showing political boundaries) or a weather map (showing cold fronts) or a vegetation map (showing type and density of flora) or a language map (showing where different language groups have congregated). Each of these maps is particularly useful for certain purposes. A political map isn't very helpful if you want to know what to wear tomorrow. And a weather map isn't terribly helpful if you're trying to find the road to Des Moines. With this in mind, let's look at the definitional maps that have been drawn for communication and more specifically for nonverbal communication.

At first, it seems it should be simple to map communication. We all communicate from birth. It is as obvious—and yet as unnoticed—as breathing. But under scrutiny, communication begins to look more complex. It is familiar but subtle. It is unique and universal. It is slippery and inescapable. It may be one person making one gesture to someone. And even that simple act is multidimensional, multifaceted, multileveled. Or it may be an ongoing code system such as a language, or music, or an art form, which lasts thousands of years and encompasses millions of people.

When we begin to draw the boundaries of communication, we are forced to ask: What precisely is it we wish to denote? What do we want to mean by "communication"? Is it something which only happens among humans? Or does it occur among animals, among insects, among computers? Does it require a "language"? And, if so, what do we mean by language? Is the honey dance of the bee a language? Does communication require both a sender and a receiver? Or is sending enough? Or receiving? Must it be done with intent? Or can we communicate unintentionally? Must it be done with awareness? Or can we be oblivious to some of the messages we send and receive? Does it involve only the content of our messages? Or does it include the many cues we use to regulate our interactions? Does it include the transmission of feelings? Or should it only deal with the rational and the cognitive?

Most of our traditional definitions of communication have focused on (a) humans, (b) verbal symbols, and (c) cognitive messages. Our models of communication have tended to be source-oriented; we see communication starting with a source who wants to get an idea across (rather than a receiver who is seeking information). Our models have been linear and one-way, with information flowing from source to receiver (rather than flowing many ways within a system). We have focused on situations in which communication is purposeful and done with intent, where the outcome involves persuasion or influence. But explorations of the nonverbal domain have challenged some of these assumptions.

Cataloging

Up to now, many writers on nonverbal communication have ducked the problem of defining the area. They have instead listed types of phenomena that should be or could be included. For example, Jurgen Ruesch and Weldon Kees, the first to use the term "nonverbal communication" in a book title, included three areas: sign language, action language, and object language.[2] *Sign language* includes the purposeful use of gesture to replace words. Examples would be the hitchhiker's thumbing or the hand signals of the deaf. *Action language* includes all movements that were not done with the express intent of communicating. For example, a young man might wolf down his food—not because he wishes to communicate but simply because he is hungry. An observer, however, might infer that

---

[2] Jurgen Ruesch and Weldon Kees, *Nonverbal Communication: Notes on the Visual Perception of Human Relations* (Berkeley, Calif.: University of California Press, 1956; 2nd ed., 1971).

he is hungry, that he had a poor upbringing, and so on. *Object language* includes both the intentional and unintentional display of material things: clothing, art objects, machines, architectural structures; it even includes the display of type and lettering.

The number of areas to be included in the nonverbal domain has ranged from 3 to 18, or more, depending on where the mapper drew the boundaries and the subdivisions. The following lists are not exciting reading, but they give you a sense of how people have viewed the field, and they suggest places you may find more information if you have a special interest.

Larry Barker and Nancy Collins identified 18 candidates for the nonverbal domain: (1) animal and insect; (2) culture; (3) environment; (4) gestural, facial expression, bodily movement, and kinesic; (5) human behavior; (6) interaction patterns; (7) learning; (8) machine; (9) media; (10) mental processes, perception, imagination, and creativity; (11) music; (12) paralinguistics; (13) personal grooming and apparel; (14) physiological; (15) pictures; (16) space; (17) tactile and cutaneous and (18) time.[3]

Abne Eisenberg and Ralph Smith use three major categories of nonverbal communication: paralanguage; kinesics, the study of body movement; and proxemics, the study of space.[4] Meanwhile, Mark Knapp organizes the nonverbal domain into (1) body motion or kinesic behavior, (2) physical characteristics, (3) touching behavior, (4) paralanguage, (5) proxemics, (6) artifacts, and (7) environmental factors.[5] Michael Argyle includes (1) bodily contact, (2) posture, (3) physical appearance, (4) facial and gestural movement, (5) direction of gaze, and (6) nonverbal aspects of speech—timing, emotional tone, and accent.[6] Finally, Starkey Duncan outlines nonverbal communication in terms of (1) body movement or kinesic behavior (e.g., gestures and other body movements, including facial expressions, eye movements, and posture); (2) paralanguage (e.g., voice qualities, speech nonfluencies, and such vocalizations as laughing, yawning, and grunting); (3) proxemics (i.e., the use of social and personal space); (4) olfaction; (5) skin sensitivity to temperature and touch; and (6) use of artifacts (e.g., dress and cosmetics).[7]

---

[3] Larry L. Barker and Nancy B. Collins, "Nonverbal and Kinesic Research," in P. Emmert and W. D. Brooks (eds.), *Methods of Research in Communication* (Boston: Houghton Mifflin, 1970), pp. 343–372.

[4] Abne M. Eisenberg and Ralph R. Smith, Jr., *Nonverbal Communication* (Indianapolis: Bobbs-Merrill, 1971).

[5] Mark L. Knapp, *Nonverbal Communication in Human Interaction* (New York: Holt, Rinehart and Winston, 1972).

[6] Michael Argyle, *Social Interaction* (Chicago: Aldine-Atherton, 1969).

[7] Starkey, Duncan, Jr., "Nonverbal Communication," *Psychological Bulletin*, 72, 1969, pp. 118–137.

These authors all agree that body movements should be included. But beyond that, they do not agree on what should be fenced in or out of the nonverbal range.

In trying to understand why different mappers have sketched different definitions of nonverbal communication, it may be helpful to explore the problems they were trying to solve; what led them to find one definition more useful than another? If you sent someone interested in mining and someone interested in agriculture to a strange land, they would probably come back with different notes; they would be looking for—and seeing—different things. So it has been when the nonverbal domain was visited by the psychologist, the anthropologist, the sociologist, the ethologist (a man who studies animal behavior), and the practitioner—the filmmaker, the counselor, the administrator.

THE ANTHROPOLOGICAL APPROACH

The anthropologist takes a broad view. He looks at whole societies. He looks at the evolution of culture over centuries. He is likely to conclude that "culture is communication." [8] If that is the case, then communication includes work, play, defense, territoriality, sex, learning, and so on. The exchange of verbal symbols between two people may be only a small part of the total communication spectrum.

The anthropologist would like to account for the pattern or structure which persists over time, even though the individuals may change. In other words, our language was here before we came. We use it while we're here. We may modify, invent, delete. But when we leave, the same language, more or less, will be going on in new generations. It is this ongoing system the anthropologist would like to understand.

Some pioneers, like Ray L. Birdwhistell, do not, in fact, like the term "nonverbal communication." They feel it makes an unnatural division in the total communication system which each child learns as he grows up. Birdwhistell uses the term *kinesics* to deal with those aspects of communication which come about through body movement. His approach to nonverbal behavior is very much like the approach of the linguist who is trying to understand and systematize any strange language.

The practical implications of the anthropological approach are widespread. Particularly in the era since World War II, the anthropologist has provided important insights for cross-cultural communication. He has helped us undestand other men in a fast-shrinking world. And he has shed light on some of the factors which make us human, wherever man is found.

[8] Edward T. Hall, *The Silent Language* (Greenwich, Conn.: Fawcett, 1959).

PSYCHOLOGICAL APPROACHES

While the anthropologist would like to extract the ongoing pattern and drop out the unique individual, the psychologist has an opposite interest. He would like to assume the cultural pattern and not study that; but he is interested in the individual. He would like to know how an individual learns his language, or any other communication behavior. He would like to explain individual differences, why some individuals (within the same culture) are one way and others are different.

Psychological definitions of communication have thus tended to focus on the individual. For example, one suggests that if any stimulus impinges on an organism, and if it elicits a response: that's communication. Some have interpreted this to mean that if the sun shines on me and I turn red, that's communication. Other psychologists have said, no, it has to be a *learned* response. If the sun shines on you and you put on suntan lotion, that's communication.

This very broad definition, of course, opens the door to many nonverbal events. Some psychologists, however, have viewed communication as primarily a verbal phenomenon. They have suggested that even when we see a nonverbal event, such as a painting, we translate the experience, inside our heads, into verbal labels; the brain, in short, processes, stores, and retrieves using "verbal mediators" or word-like tags.

While this view has been popular in American psychology, a totally opposing view states that information processing in the brain is completely different from the verbal languages men use between themselves. Rather, this position argues, what happens in the head is essentially a nonverbal process, involving imagery and perhaps something like holography, the modern technology which produces three-dimensional pictures. A third, and increasingly popular position, suggests that the brain works both verbally and nonverbally. It is very facile at converting information from one mode to the other, although some individuals may be better "nonverbal thinkers" while others shine as "verbal thinkers."

Intent

Ever since Freud, psychologists have wrestled with conscious and unconscious intent, the degree to which an individual is aware of what he's doing and why. What if an artist, without realizing it, fills his paintings with phallic symbols: is that communication? Or what if he has read Freud, and is doing it on purpose? And in either case, does there have to be a receiver who responds before we have full communication? And how aware does this receiver have to be? Is it only communication if the viewer is a psychiatrist, who is fully aware of all the phallic symbols and their import? Or how about the young woman who is strangely moved by the painting but does not realize that phallic symbolism is involved?

Focusing on this frequent problem in the study of nonverbal cues, Paul Ekman and Wallace Friesen have distinguished three levels: behaviors that are (a) *informative*, (b) *interactive*, or (c) *communicative*.[9] If, for example, our young woman blushed while looking at the paintings, this might be *informative* to an observer. The woman did not intend to "communicate" about her embarrassment; but an observer sees a cue which informs him about some inner state. Similarly, if the psychiatrist notes the symbols in the painting, and makes some inferences about the painter, that is informative.

Some cues may be *interactive* in that they influence the interaction. Someone, seeing the young woman's blush, might decide he would like to interact with such a nice, modest person. Someone else might decide just the opposite. More typically, we engage in a whole range of nonverbal behaviors, such as head nods, eye contact, and smiling, which have a strong impact on human interaction. Yet they appear to be performed with little awareness or intent on the part of the sender; and they are reacted to with little awareness on the part of the receiver.

Finally, Ekman and Friesen reserve the term *communicative* for those behaviors that are done with an intent to communicate. If the painter purposefully inserts his phallic symbolism, that's "communicative" (whether anyone else interprets it or not). If he does not do it with intent, then it still may be "informative" (to the psychiatrist), or it may be "interactive" (to the blushing maiden who turns away). But it would not be "communicative."

THE MIDDLE GROUND

Between the anthropologist and the psychologist is the sociologist, the social psychologist, and others, such as the clinician working with family therapy. Where the psychologist might be willing to define communication in terms of a single individual, either a sender or a receiver, these researchers usually want at least two communicators. And they want some degree of interaction or transaction. One approach suggests that whenever you are in the presence of another person, "You cannot *not* communicate."[10] No matter what you do, you are sending the other person *some* message. And his reaction, whatever it is, sends a message back to you. Even silence and rigid inactivity may tell your partner that you are angry, depressed, hostile, fearful, annoyed. Here, obviously, non-

[9] Paul Ekman and Wallace V. Friesen, "The Repertoire of Nonverbal Behavior: Categories, Origins, Usage, and Coding," *Semiotica*, 1, 1969, pp. 49–98.
[10] Paul Watzlawick, J. H. Beavin, and D. D. Jackson, *Pragmatics of Human Communication* (New York: W. W. Norton, 1967).

verbal activity is taken as part of communication, and intent is not seen as a prerequisite, you may communicate whether you intend to or not.

Sociologists, Erving Goffman, for instance, have been interested in the ritual that individuals go through in forming and maintaining relationships.[11] Social psychologists, Albert Mehrabian, for instance, have looked at the dimensions of these relationships and how they are communicated. Mehrabian sees the transmission of feeling as the crucial function of nonverbal communication.[12] In forming and maintaining relationships, he sees three major dimensions: (a) the *immediacy* dimension, the communication of liking–disliking; (b) the *power* dimension, the communication of status, dominance, and submission; and (c) the *responsiveness* dimension, the communication of awareness and reaction. He argues that these major messages may be communicated with a variety of nonverbal behaviors: body movement, posture, eye contact, head nods, smiles, and so on.

Recently, the nonverbal domain has been enriched with the viewpoint of ethologists, men who have been studying the social behavior of animals.[13] Ethologists' interest goes back to the time of Charles Darwin, who is seen by some as the father of modern, scientific, nonverbal communication.[14] Darwin, just over one hundred years ago, examined nonverbal expressions of man in relation to the behavior of animals. Many of his observations, long ignored, are now, a century later, being recognized as powerful insights.

In summary, the modern study of nonverbal communication draws on a rich history of exploration, from many investigators from many intellectual homelands. The different mappings of the nonverbal domain may at first be confusing. But it is also illuminating to have so many perspectives. Each provides a useful frame for predictions about communication behavior, as we will see in Chapter 5. And the activity of so many researchers testifies to the broad implications of nonverbal communication. Man's use of nonverbal symbols is important, no matter how you look at it.

You have been so enthralled with this account that you forgot where you were. But suddenly, a deep voice says: "We are disappointed in you, Earthling. We thought because you were read-

---

[11] Erving Goffman, *Relations in Public* (New York: Basic Books, 1971).

[12] Albert Mehrabian, *Nonverbal Communication* (Chicago: Aldine-Atherton, 1972).

[13] Robert A. Hinde, *Non-verbal Communication* (New York: Cambridge University Press, 1972).

[14] Charles Darwin, *The Expression of the Emotions in Man and Animals* (London: John Murray, 1872; Chicago: University of Chicago Press, 1965).

ing that book you were an expert in nonverbal communication. But you do not appear to understand our symbols. We are sending you back."

Quickly, you ask: "What does the '+' mean?"

The voice responds: "You must understand that, for our Beings, one walking limb is shorter than the other. That is why our floors are slanted. What appears to you as '+' is really '×'."

Then, before you have a chance to ask another question, you are engulfed in a white light. And you are back in your study.

Moral Number One: Don't gaze at the stars when you should be studying this book.

Moral Number Two: Hurry up and finish the book before that white light comes back again.

DISCUSSION–EXERCISES

1. Imagine you are designing a message for a deep space probe—a message that might be found by some Other Intelligence. What would your message look like? What assumptions are you making?

2. On their way to a neighborhood bar, six men pass a mark on the wall that looks like this: ℶ.

(a) Abe doesn't see it; (b) Barney sees it but decides it's an accidental scratch; (c) Carl sees it and concludes it's meaningful—but doesn't know what it could mean; (d) Desmond sees it and concludes it's an Indian good luck sign; (e) Ephraim sees it, concludes it's a swastika, and he's appalled; (f) Ferdinand sees it, concludes it's a swastika, and thinks it's great (he's a Fascist).

They then all gather at the bar and begin discussing the mark. (If you have six friends or classmates, this is fun to role-play.) What will happen? Which two will have most difficulty getting together? Can you diagram their problems in the decision tree of Figure 2-1?

3. In predicting or explaining communication behavior, when might you want to take an anthropological perspective? A psychological approach? An approach from the middle ground?

SYSTEMS

3

communication
systems

LEARNING TIPS

This is a "heavy" chapter, designed to give you a fast but fairly thorough overview of "systems" terminology. This viewpoint, in turn, provides the foundation for analyzing complex communication situations—and the complex codes men use in their attempts to understand each other.

In this chapter you will be introduced to the following concepts:

- system
- suprasystem
- subsystem
- component
- levels
- boundary
- environment
- system states
- interface
- physical systems
- energy systems
- information systems
- code
- structure
- function
- evolution
- formation stage
- operation stage
- maintenance
- productivity
- termination stage
- communicator roles
- decoder
- processor
- encoder
- systems administrator
- ABX-X' model
- coding dimension
- relationship dimension

THOUGHT STARTERS

1. When you have a communication problem now, how do you go about analyzing it?

2. Review the above terms; how many do you have a meaning for now?

Al looks at his roommate. Bill hasn't shaved in three days. His desk is in disarray. His posture, his clothes, his facial expression—everything bespeaks of sadness. He just hasn't been the same since Mims left town. Al looks at his watch. He clears his throat. Bill looks up from his book.

Smiling, Al says, "I met a very interesting girl last night."

"That's nice," says Bill flatly, and returns to the book.

Moving closer, Al says, "You'd like her" . . . Bill looks up, eyebrows raised quizzically . . . "She's just your type," Al adds, making an hourglass figure in the air with his hands.

"That's nice . . . ," says Bill, shaking his head. "But that's your type," he points toward Al. "I like them with something up here," he adds, tapping his forehead.

THIS BRIEF ENCOUNTER BETWEEN TWO ROOMMATES introduces us to an ongoing communication *system*. What do we mean by "system"? A *system* is a *set of interrelated elements*. There must be (a) elements, and (b) relationships. Al and Bill are elements in this communication system; they are related by the messages they exchange.

In this chapter we will introduce you to the problems of being a good systems analyst, the problems of diagnosing effective (and ineffective) communication situations. This is the first step in becoming an effective systems administrator, an individual who can create and maintain effective communication systems.

In the first two chapters we looked at the problems of nonverbal communication largely from the perspective of a decoder, a receiver of nonverbal cues. In the "Right"–"Right" cartoon, you were asked to interpret the nonverbal events you saw. In your adventure in outer space, you took an even closer look at the process, and problems, of decoding even a single, simple nonverbal sign. Now we want to introduce you to other roles you play in nonverbal communication, the role of encoder as well as decoder, the role of information processor, and, finally, the role of systems administrator. But for these roles, you will need a new toolkit of terms, a vocabulary to help you see, analyze, diagnose.

COMMUNICATION SYSTEMS

The illustrations on the following pages provide some nonverbal as well as verbal elaboration of key systems terms.

Boundaries/Environment

Figure 3-1 suggests that systems can be separated from their *environment* by a *boundary*. With physical systems, this boundary is often obvious. The skin is the physical boundary of the human body. The boundaries of communication systems are sometimes harder to identify. The nonverbal literature, for instance, suggests that we walk around with a "bubble of personal space," a region of psychological territory which is within the boundary of our "self" system. If people come too close, they violate this invisible system boundary. In the example of Al and Bill, they are elements in a common communication system. Al's new acquaintance is outside the system—in the "environment"—at least for the moment. Bill and his book define another communication system. Al is outside the boundary of that system.

FIGURE 3-1   System Boundaries.

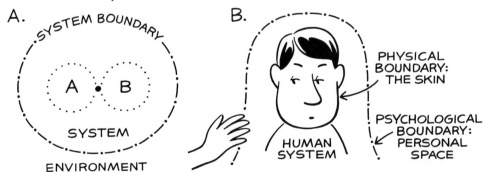

A. Diagram of a simple system with two elements, A and B, linked by one relationship.

B. The human system. The skin defines one boundary, the physical. But the "self" may be defined by other boundaries, e.g., a bubble of personal space.

Suprasystem, System, Subsystem, Component

Figure 3-2 indicates that systems can be analyzed at *levels*. The level we are primarily interested in is called the *system*. But the system may, in turn, be made up of several *subsystems*. These subsystems may be made up of subsubsystems—which, in turn, could be made up of subsub-subsystems, and so on. The elements in our lowest level of analysis are called *components*.

Moving in the other direction, our system may be part of a sub-system in some larger *suprasystem*. In the example of Al and Bill, their living space represents a system that is within a larger suprasystem: an apartment building, a dormitory, a fraternity house, a coop, a rooming house. This suprasystem may, in turn, be a system within a larger supra-system: an apartment complex, the dormitory system, the fraternity sys-tem, the off-campus living system. The living area may, in turn, be divided up into subsystems, such as kitchen, bathroom, bedroom. Or we

FIGURE 3-2   System Levels.

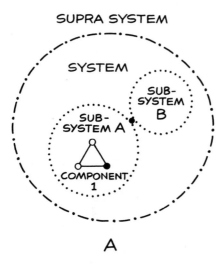

A   B

A. A diagram of a system (within a suprasystem). The system has two sub-systems. And one of these subsystems has three components.

B. The human is made up of several subsystems: the central nervous system, the cardiovascular system, the gastro-intestinal system, and so on. In turn, these subsystems have subsystems. For example, the heart is a component of the cardiovascular system.

might consider other subsystems: the electrical system, the plumbing system, the heating system. Avid television viewers are, of course, familiar with the important subsystems of the human body, such as the gastro-intestinal system and the sinus system.

System States

Figure 3-3 illustrates the concept of system *states*. A system, or a subsystem, can be in different states, or conditions. And frequently it is important to note the state or states of a system if we are to accurately predict outcomes. Some simple systems have only two states, such as "on"–"off" or "full"–"empty." We also speak of humans as being "turned on" or "turned off." We speak of them as being "full"—of food—or other substances. But the human communicator can exist in a wide range of cognitive and emotional states.

Returning to Al and Bill, Al is in a state of "concern" about his roommate, who appears to be in a state of "sadness." This leads him to

FIGURE 3-3 System States.

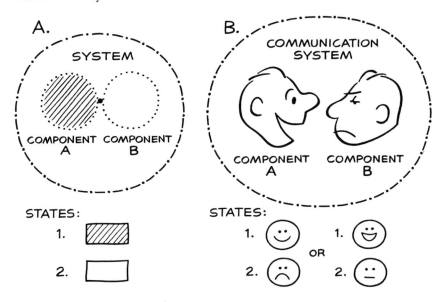

A. A system with two components. Each component is in a different state. The system state is defined by the states of the components: A-1 and B-2.

B. A human communication system. The human components also exhibit "states." A is talking. B is listening. A is happy. B is not happy.

move to a state of communication. He becomes a speaker and Bill becomes a listener. Then Bill adopts the speaker state, and Al is the listener. At the same time, they are in states with respect to their nonverbal communication: sending, not sending; receiving, not receiving.

Interface

Figure 3-4 illustrates the concept of *interface,* the link which joins components. It is through this interface that components are related. In *physical systems,* such as a plumbing system, the interface provides a flow of matter, such as water. In *energy systems,* such as an electrical system, the interface permits the flow of energy, such as electricity, between components. In *information systems,* such as two men talking, the interface provides the flow of messages. In the information interface, some matter or energy is required, for example, light or sound waves or the pressure of touch. But the information component does not change states simply because of the matter or energy transmitted. Rather, these small amounts of matter or energy provide information.

In the case of Al and Bill, they do not touch—although Al may feel

FIGURE 3-4 (Part I)   System Interface.

A. PHYSICAL SYSTEM

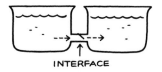

INTERFACE

B. ENERGY SYSTEM

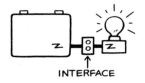

INTERFACE

C. INFORMATION SYSTEM

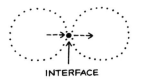

INTERFACE

This diagram illustrates three systems: (a) a physical system, such as a hydraulic system; (b) an energy system, such as a battery and light bulb; and (c) an information system, such as two computers chatting.

Figure 3-4 (Part II)   System Interface.

The human communicator is an information system with many "interfaces."
He can receive messages from other communicators by touch, taste, smell,
sight, and sound.

like slugging his slovenly roommate. But their sense receptors pick up
the variations in light and sound created by behavior. Bill hears Al clear
his throat—and Bill looks up. Al sees how Bill looks and he infers how
Bill is feeling.

Codes

Figure 3-5 highlights the concept of *code*. Information systems are
able to operate on low levels of matter and energy because these small
units of matter or energy are *coded*: they stand for something else. They
mean something beyond the sheer magnitude of their physical power. In
an electrical system, if we want a light bulb to turn on, we have to
provide all the necessary energy from some other component in the system,
such as a battery or a generator. But a human communicator may be
"turned on" by the soft words "I love you" or "You're beautiful."

How many codes are Al and Bill using? They are linked by two interfaces, the channels of sight and sound. But in each channel are several
codes. Some are simple, with few elements and an uncomplicated structure among elements. Others are complex, with many elements and involved structures. We might consider shaving as a code that is informative. Bill has shaved or he hasn't shaved. And if he hasn't, it's been a
period of days, or months, or years. On the other hand, the phrase "That's
nice," contains several sounds—several code elements—and a very complex

FIGURE 3-5   Communication Codes.

This information system uses a simple binary code: either "1" or "0." Even a two-element code system can have complex relationships, however, as in modern computer applications.

The human communicator can process many codes at each interface, each sensory modality. These codes are often complicated, with many possible elements and many complex interrelationships.

order. A communicator has to learn much about the linguistic code system before he can accurately decode Bill's flat statement.

SYSTEMS IN ACTION

The systems terminology is useful in analyzing communication situations because it allows us to see similarities. Rather than each situation emerging as unique, we can see patterns which repeat again and again. It helps us understand and predict. As a first step, communication systems can be grouped according to (a) *structure*, (b) *function*, and (c) *evolution*.

Structure

Figure 3-6 illustrates the concept of *structure*. Systems may differ in that they have few components or many. An army has many components,

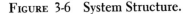

FIGURE 3-6   System Structure.

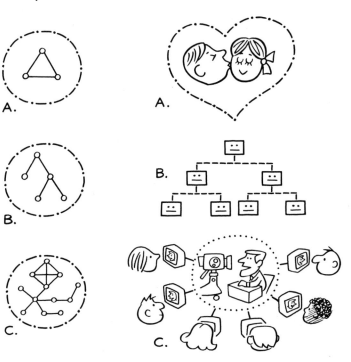

System structure may differ in (a) the number of components, and (b) the way those components are interrelated. System A has fewer components than B or C, but it is fully interconnected. B has more components, but not as many as C. In C's case, part of the system is richly interconnected and part is not.

Human systems similarly differ in size and interrelationships. In A the young lovers want only each other in their system. And they want their "interconnectedness" as rich as possible. In B a business organization may have daily meetings, phone connections, and inter-office memos. But there may also be a strict hierarchy. In a mass-media system (C) audience members may be scattered across space and time, with little contact among themselves.

many individuals. Meanwhile, Al and Bill have only two individuals in their communications system. Systems also differ in the complexity of the interrelationships among components. Some systems have many levels: systems, subsystems, and subsubsystems. Other systems merely have a set of components all on the same level. An army, for example, has several levels in its hierarchy. But Al and Bill are equals. Some systems have a rich interrelationship among components; other systems have looser interconnections. In an army, the links are carefully delimited: the private talks to the sergeant who in turn talks to the lieutenant. Meanwhile, in their systems, Al and Bill interact frequently and they feel free to chat about anything.

Function

Figure 3-7 illustrates the concept of *function*. Communication systems come into being—and are likely to be continued—because they serve some function, for someone. They fulfill a need, a purpose, a goal. Sometimes, the system serves a function for the larger environment. A newspaper functions to inform its public. Second, the system may serve itself. The newspaper earns revenue from its output and this allows it to continue. Finally, the system may serve its components. By his activities, the re-

FIGURE 3-7   System Functions.

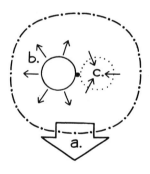 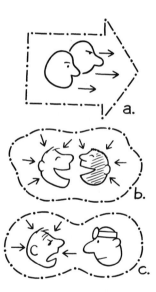

Functions of a system. The activities of a system may serve (a) the larger environment or suprasystem, (b) the system itself, (c) one or more of the components, or (d) any combination of (a), (b), and (c).

In human communication systems, (a) people may work together to accomplish a larger outside goal. Or (b) they may engage in purely social activity, which is enjoyable to the participants. Or (c) they may work to help one of the participants, as in a doctor–patient interaction.

porter earns wages. The owner derives a profit. Advertisers sell goods. Systems that fulfill needs at all three levels are likely to survive. Those that fill needs at only one level may be more vulnerable. Within any communication system, of course, a large number of needs may be served. The functions of a doctor–patient interview are different from the interaction of a salesman and his prospect, Al and his roommate, a student and an instructor, a policeman and a motorist, or Bill and a date.

Evolution

Figure 3-8 illustrates the concept of system *evolution*. Even when we find two systems which are similar in structure and function, we may discover that they have evolved differently. Hence, they may be on different trajectories into the future. Some communication systems come into being, are very intense for a period, but then fade away. Others may be

FIGURE 3-8   **System Evolution.**

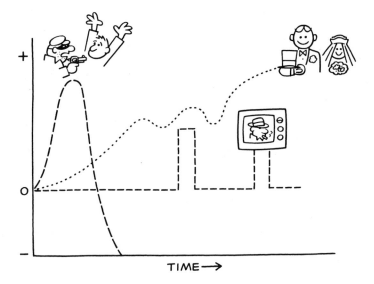

Some communication systems, such as a holdup, last a short time, involve intense interaction, and, one hopes, do not recur. Others, such as a romance, may build up slowly but continue over a long period of time. And some communication systems are intermittent, like a weekly television show, or an old friend seen occasionally.

less intense but longer lasting. And many communication systems have cycles of activity and inactivity. Al and Bill have obviously interacted many times before. As roommates, they have an ongoing communication system. And as we looked in on them, they were once again reactivating their system.

Evolution refers to the long-range history of a system: its growth and development, its expansion and perhaps eventual decline. Within evolution, or even within the shorter cycles of activation, we can often see distinct stages: (a) the *formation* stage; (b) the *operation* stage, with its activities devoted to *maintenance* and *productivity*; and (c) the *termination* stage, when the system is deactivated or closed down.

The Formation Stage

In the first stage, communicators become aware of each other and the possibility of communicating. They exchange glances. They smile. In the case of Al, he cleared his throat, and Bill looked up. Or, in scanning the mass media, we may be attracted by a fetching picture, an unusual layout, a colorful design, or captivating music.

There is, in short, the realization that interesting messages may be available to us. And during the formation stage, we may make some assessment of just how rewarding those messages will be. We also may assess how costly. How much time and energy will it take to interact with that person, or read that book, or watch that show? We may have to weigh the rewards and costs of one communication system against another. (Do you want to read tonight so you can pass that exam—or do you want to go to the flicks, which would be more fun—at least in the short run?)

If the communicators decide to interact, a "formation ritual" follows. We have to be sure the other person wants to interact with us. We have to set up the rules for the communication system we are launching. In social settings, there are often nonverbal cues to be exchanged: an appropriate handshake, a bow, a curtsy, a properly placed kiss. Only after we have duly acknowledged the other person can we get down to the business of our interaction.

The Operation Stage: Production and Maintenance

Once launched, the communication system (a) moves toward goals, and (b) works to maintain itself. The first involves "productivity"— what is it the interaction hopes to produce? Two workmen may meet to solve a problem. Or a patient sees a doctor, hoping to be cured. Sometimes, of course, the only goal is to have a good time, to enjoy the other person's company, or to be amused by that TV show.

If a communication system is trying to solve problems, tensions may arise. First, the communicators may have difficulty deciding just what the interaction should produce. Then comes the difficult task of producing. As tension rises, the communicators may exchange angry looks. An edge of sarcasm may creep into the voice. They may make movements of withdrawal. Al, for example, had trouble keeping Bill engaged in conversation. Bill said "That's nice," perhaps sarcastically, and turned back to his book.

If the tensions and frictions in a system are left unattended, the system will fly apart. Messages must be exchanged that reassure the participants. They may need to know they are appreciated, that the system will produce a worthwhile outcome, that they will be rewarded. Frequently, this maintenance activity takes place through a flow of nonverbal cues, positive expressions of emotion, smiles, head nods, touching looks indicating that the person is receiving attention. In the mass media, the communicator may have to introduce other cues that reward the audience, novel cues to combat boredom, or illustrations that make the material easier to understand or more fun to deal with. Finally, when the communicators have reached their goals—or exhausted their willingness to work toward those goals—they are ready for the "termination ritual" (see Figure 3-9).

The Termination Stage

In the termination stage, the communicators engage in various rituals to "tie off" the interaction. Or, in mass-media messages, there is an attempt to wrap up, create closure, but also set the stage for "next time." In face-to-face interaction, there are usually three steps: (a) signaling the desire to leave, (b) granting permission to leave, and (c) the actual farewell ritual. The desire to leave may be signaled nonverbally, with a glance at your watch, a movement toward the door, a gathering up of possessions. This may be accompanied by a half-finished verbal statement indicating that you "gotta go (mumble, mumble). . . ." Unless the other communicator is completely absorbed in his topic or misses your cues, he is then obligated to "grant permission" for your leave taking. Often, this comes in the form of a counterrequest: "Yeah, I gotta run along, too. . . ."

The farewell ritual may be very formal, requiring a handshake and other termination gestures. Or, in many cases, it can be relatively informal: a nod, a smile, a wave, a flash of the eyebrows. While the farewell ritual

FIGURE 3-9   System Formation, Operation, and Termination.

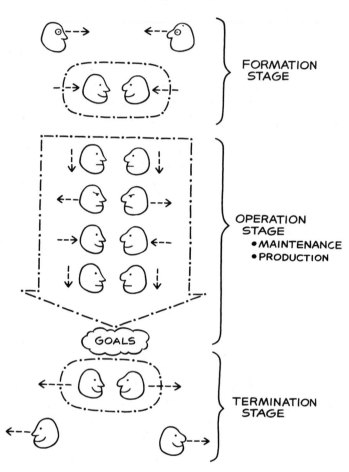

Communication systems move through stages of (a) formation; (b) operation, with maintenance and achievement; and (c) termination.

may be quite brief, it is usually important—especially if you ever hope to interact with that individual again. To check the importance of the termination stage, end a phone conversation by simply hanging up on a friend without saying "good-bye." Usually, if the other person isn't angered beyond response, he'll call back and ask, "Were we cut off?"

Again, in the termination stage, nonverbal cues can play a significant role. They often signal the desire to leave. And typically, the farewell ritual requires some appropriate nonverbal interaction along with the verbal statements.

As communicators, within communication systems, we play three major roles: (a) we are *decoders,* or receivers of messages; (b) we are *processors* of messages, relating, storing, retrieving, creating; and (c) we are *encoders,* or sources of messages (Figure 3-10). Finally, we play a fourth role: we are *administrators* of communication systems. We try to create and activate and maintain effective communication systems around ourselves. And we try to organize systems for others who decode, process, and encode.

In large, formal communication systems, each of these roles may be a full-time task. But in our small, day-to-day systems, we play all of these

FIGURE 3-10   Communicator Roles.

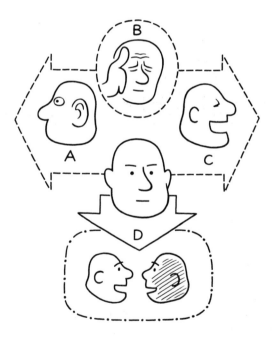

The modern communicator plays many roles within communication systems: he is (a) decoder, (b) processor, (c) encoder, and (d) systems administrator.

roles, often simultaneously, or in quick succession. In particular, we may get help in encoding verbal messages, in courses in speech and writing. Increasingly, youngsters are also being tutored in the production of nonverbal messages: painting, sculpture, music, photography, dance. On the decoding side, we may find courses in rapid reading, or listening skills, or in art and music appreciation.

In some areas communication management skills have also been codified and taught. There are techniques of systems management for the psychiatrist, the counselor, the professional interviewer, the journalist, the salesman, the conference leader. Courses have been organized around parliamentary procedure, Robert's Rules of Order, small-group leadership. But typically, we are least aware of our role as "communication executive." We may be least aware of how to tackle that role effectively.

THE ABX-X' MODEL OF COMMUNICATION

To be more effective in our communication roles, we may need—at least at times—to be analytic. We need to be able to sort out what is going on. We need to diagnose problems and spot possible solutions. This is especially true with nonverbal communication, which is often subtle but powerful, operating at low levels of awareness for both the decoder and the encoder.

Unfortunately, many of our classic models of communication do not place communication within a systems context. They do not point to two important dimensions of communication: how people relate, and how they encode messages about events in the environment. To spotlight these dimensions, we will want to expand our earlier A-M-B model (communicators A and B exchanging messages). We will build, instead, on the A-B-X model of Theodore Newcomb.[1]

In Newcomb's model, A and B are communicators, exchanging messages about some X—a referent, some object, event or person in the environment. We will want to complicate this model in one respect. We want to call attention to the messages about X. And we will call these messages X' (X-prime).

To pick up our example of Al and Bill, Al would be represented by A and Bill would be represented by B. The girl Al knows is—for now—simply the mysterious Miss X. And the messages exchanged about Ms. X will be labeled X'.

As the ABX-X' model is diagrammed (Figure 3-11) we see two major dimensions: (a) the *coding dimension*, the vertical line linking mes-

---

[1] Theodore M. Newcomb, "An Approach to the Study of Communicative Acts," *Psychological Review*, 60, 1953, pp. 393–404.

FIGURE 3-11   The ABX-X' Model of Communication.

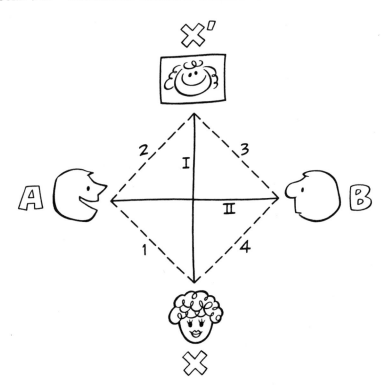

Communicator A encodes a message (X') about event (X) for communicator B. Dimension I is the coding dimension. Dimension II is the relationship dimension. Peripheral dimensions are (1) perception; (2) encoding; (3) decoding, and (4) response.

sages and the events they represent; and (b) the *relationship dimension,* the horizontal line linking the two communicators.

The Coding Dimension

Frequently, we pay little attention to *how* events in the environment are encoded into messages. But the X-to-X' dimension reminds us that, when we are communicating to humans, we can use many different codes. Al can refer to his acquaintance as "a girl" (using a verbal label), or he can make a gesture with his hands (a nonverbal sign), or he might show Bill a picture (a graphic nonverbal sign). Some of these coding choices will be more effective than others. Some will take more time and effort on the part of the encoder. Some will demand more energy from the decoder. In short, the coding choices will have an impact on the effectiveness and efficiency of the communication system.

The Relationship Dimension

When we analyze a communication system, we are usually immediately aware of what is being "talked about." We know that X is being discussed. But we are usually less aware of the messages A and B exchange about themselves and about their mutual communication system. Yet without these messages, the communication system could not operate. The communicators have to decide how they are going to relate, who is going to speak when, how they are going to regulate their system. They have to be able to send messages of interest or disinterest, indications of excitement or boredom, cues of sincerity or joking. To be effective with his roommate, Al will have to send messages about himself, how he feels about Bill, and how he feels about their interaction. These messages will prove to be as important as his messages about X.

Collapsing this back into our A-M-B model, we can state that the message component contains four sets of messages: (a) X', the messages about events X in the environment; (b) A', messages about communicator A; (c) B', messages about communicator B; and (d) $A'B'$, messages about the communincators' relationship, about their joint communication system. The first set of messages deals with events outside the communication system. The other messages deal with events inside the communication system. In each case, these messages may be encoded in verbal signs (Sv) or nonverbal signs (Snv) (see Figure 3-12).

SUMMARY

This chapter provides the foundation for future analysis of communication systems. The terms introduced here are useful in examining man's interactions. In Chapter 4 these terms will be applied again, this time to the systems of signs which man has at his disposal in his attempt to understand and be understood.

System was defined as an interrelated set of elements. Systems have *levels*, including: *suprasystems*, the level above the system; and *subsystems*, the level below the system. The elements at the lowest level of analysis are called *components*. Systems have *boundaries*, which separate the system from its *environment*. Where two systems join, we have an *interface*. In information systems, such as human communication, messages flow across the interface; small units of matter or energy are coded to

FIGURE 3-12   The Message Components.

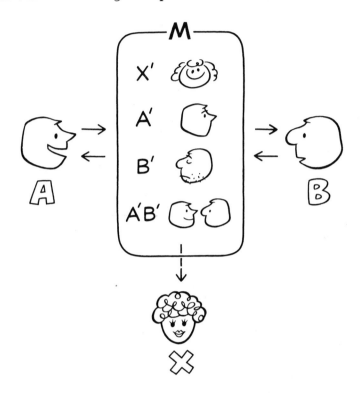

The message components may include four sets of messages: (a) **X'**, messages about external events; (b) **A'**, messages about communicator A; (c) **B'**, messages about communicator B; and (d) **A'B'**, messages about the relationship of the two communicators.

provide *information*. In analyzing communication systems, we may also need to know the *states* of the system, the possible states that could exist as well as the condition of the system at present.

Systems may differ in *structure, function,* and *evolution*. Structure is determined by the number of elements and their interconnections. Function deals with the purposes served by the system, for the larger environment, for the system itself, for the components. Through time, a system may move through stages: the *formation* stage, the *operation* stage, and the *termination* stage. During the operation stage, the system may be balanced between the forces of *productivity* and *maintenance*.

Within communication systems, we play several roles, as *decoder, pro-*

cessor, encoder, and as systems *administrator.* In particular, we may be decoding, processing, and encoding two types of messages: messages about the environment outside the communication system, and messages about the communication system. The ABX-X′ model draws attention to (a) the *coding dimension,* the link between signs and environmental events; and (b) the *relationship dimension,* including the messages each communicator sends out about himself, his fellow communicator, and their mutual communication system. We conclude that messages can deal with (a) events inside their communication system, and (b) events outside their communication system; and either type of message may be encoded in (a) verbal signs, (b) nonverbal signs, or (c) a combination.

DISCUSSION—EXERCISES

1. Review the concepts at the beginning of the chapter. How many do you feel you understand now? If there are some you do not understand, where does the communication problem lie? How would you analyze that situation?

2. This has been a fairly "heavy" chapter in information load. To what extent have the nonverbal illustrations lightened that load? How have they done that? Are there instances where the illustrations have introduced confusion or other problems?

3. Diagram the communication system where you live.

4. How many communication systems do you engage in during a typical day?

5. Pick a communication system that is important to you. Analyze its (a) structure, (b) function, and (c) evolution. Then analyze the (a) coding dimension, and (b) the relationship dimension.

4

code systems

This is another "heavy" chapter, designed to introduce you to the terminology used in analyzing nonverbal signs and codes. It will

1. Introduce you to two major strategies of coding: the analogic and the digital.

2. Introduce you to types of *sign,* including *signals* and *symbols.*

3. Introduce you to four types of nonverbal codes: (a) performance codes, (b) artifactual codes, (c) spatio-temporal codes, and (d) mediatory codes.

4. Help you understand the following major concepts:

   - syntactic rules
   - semantic rules
   - digital
   - analogic
   - iconicity
   - marker

   - sign vehicle
   - sign
   - signal
   - symbol
   - sign patterns
   - kinesics

   - proxemics
   - performance codes
   - artifactual codes
   - spatio-temporal codes
   - mediatory codes

5. Introduce you to additional, related concepts:

   - structural meaning
   - discrete
   - continuous
   - arbitrary
   - symptom
   - index
   - linguistics
   - phone

   - allophone
   - phoneme
   - morpheme
   - kine
   - natural
   - icon
   - schematic
   - abstraction

   - allokine
   - kineme
   - kinemorph
   - primary message systems
   - isolates
   - sets
   - patterns
   - behavioreme

THOUGHT STARTERS

1. Is one picture worth a thousand words? Why? Why not?
2. In what ways do verbal and nonverbal codes differ?

Al puts his hand on Bill's shoulder and says, "Bill, I think you ought to get out a little . . . meet some new people. . . ."

Bill grunts.

Silence. Al returns to his desk.

Then Bill mumbles, "What do I want to meet new people for?"

"I don't have to draw you a picture," Al says, an edge of irritation creeping into his voice. Then, more gently, "Come on, Bill, you've been moping around here long enough."

Bill sighs. Finally, he looks up and says, "What's her name?"

"Xantippe."

"Xantippe?" says Bill, eyebrows raising. "That's a funny name!"

"She's a funny girl," says Al, quickly adding, "But you would like her." He glances at Bill, who looks thoughtful. Al then fumbles with the papers on his desk as if preparing to go to work.

After a moment's silence, Bill shrugs. "She probably wouldn't like me anyway."

"Well, she might . . . if you took a bath, and rented a tux."

"Ah, it's been so long since I've been out with a girl I wouldn't even know what to do. . . ."

"Well, you might take her down to the pool hall and shoot a few rounds with the fellows."

Bill taps his fingers thoughtfully on the arm of his chair. He begins to smile. Then he frowns. Finally, he says, "What if we got together and I just didn't like her? Or, worse, what if she didn't like me?"

"She's a liberated woman," says Al, reassuringly. "She'd probably just give you a bus token and send you home."

AL HAS GOALS IN THIS COMMUNICATION SYSTEM. He wants to cheer up his roommate. He may also just want to get him out of the house so he doesn't have to look at him. If Al were big enough, he might be able to throw his roommate out bodily. But instead, he encodes messages—small patterns of light and sound that will affect his roommate. First, he has to select a code (or codes) that his roommate understands. Then he has to select the right elements in that code—the ones which will interest, intrigue, influence. As he encodes, he also decodes; he tries to understand what Bill is thinking and feeling. In both his encoding and decoding, he is also acting as a systems administrator. He has to maintain Bill's interest. Initially, Bill seemed disinterested, and Al forced the interaction. He moved closer physically. He gestured. He encoded a verbal message calculated to hook Bill's attention. Once he caught Bill's interest, he was able to pull back. He made motions as if to leave the interaction. He let Bill take the lead.

In addition to managing their immediate communication system, the roommates are wrestling with a possible system in the future, Bill's meeting with Xantippe.

They are concerned with its formation. How will the participants get together? Will they like each other enough to actually interact? Once rolling, what is this proposed system going to do? What is it going to accomplish? How is it going to maintain itself? And, finally, how is it going to terminate? How are the participants going to get out of the system when they want out?

Bill will be in the future system. As a male on a date, he will bear some responsibility for managing the system in certain areas. But Al is also serving, indirectly, as a systems manager. He is influencing the "who" of the system. He's setting it up with Bill and Xantippe as the participants. He's influencing the "why" of the system, the goals it will have. He may even be influencing the "what" of the system, what will be discussed, what will be done. And he may help structure the "how" of the system, how the participants will relate, how they will deal with communication content.

Al's goals may seem simple: he wants Bill to cheer up, clean up, and get out. But to reach those goals, he engages in a complex communication system; and he has to plan and launch still another communication system in the future. And, to be effective in these systems, he has to select and use a complex set of messages. In this chapter we will take a closer look at the way those messages are created. We will examine, first, the requirements for a human code system. Then we'll explore two broad strategies of coding, the analogic and the digital. We'll look next at how man learns his code systems. Then we'll compare verbal and nonverbal code systems. And, finally we'll look at a broad classification of nonverbal codes:

(a) performance codes, (b) artifactual codes, (c) spatio-temporal codes, and (d) mediatory codes.

REQUIREMENTS FOR A CODE

In most cultures man speaks one language. But at the same time, he produces many nonverbal codes. Some are very complex, rivaling speech. Others are very simple, with few code elements and few rules of interrelationship. To create a code, man can use any stimulation which he can control. He can pound on a tom-tom—or on a piano. He can make puffs of smoke, or an electronic impulse. He can paint a canvas, or his face.

In short, the basic requirements for a code are (a) some stimulus which is above the sensory threshold of a human receptor, and (b) the ability to control the stimulus (e.g., turn it on or off, present it or take it away). Man can create codes for the eye, codes for the nose, codes for the ear, codes for the skin of the body or tongue of the mouth. As long as he can introduce variation into the stimulus, he can create code units, or code elements.

Beyond the basic patterning of stimulation, codes usually have two sets of rules: (a) *syntactic rules*, which decree how the code elements will be interrelated to each other (i.e., the syntactic rules tell us how the code will be organized); and (b) *semantic rules*, which relate the code to outside events (i.e., the semantic rules will tell us what the code elements will refer to, what they will "mean").

Some codes have several levels of organization. For example, the letters of the alphabet are combined, according to certain rules, to produce words. Other rules provide for the combination of words into phrases and sentences. We can, in fact, apply to codes some of the concepts we learned in Chapter 3. We can examine codes as "systems." This page is part of a larger system called a chapter, which in turn belongs to a suprasystem called "book." The page also has subsystems, such as paragraphs. And the paragraphs have subsytems, sentences, which in turn have subsystems, the words, which are in turn comprised of sets of components, the letters.

Similarly, some code systems have very complex semantic rules. We have already noted how a word, or a nonverbal sign such as "$+$," may denote a referent, some person or object. In verbal codes, the way words are strung together also introduces a type of meaning: *structural* meaning. The sentence "The boy downed the beer" has a somewhat different meaning from "The beer downed the boy." The individual words, such as "beer" and "boy," do not change their denotative meaning. But the order of the words does make a difference; two quite different (or perhaps succeeding) events are described. Similarly, as my banker keeps telling me, 73 is not the same as 37. And $7 - 3$ is not the same as $3 - 7$. The structure of the code elements makes a difference.

DIGITAL VERSUS ANALOGIC CODING

As we examine human code systems, we can note two major strategies of coding: the *digital* and the *analogic*. In an analogic system, the code elements are (a) continuous and (b) natural. The code bears a similarity to the referents. At least some of the code elements or relationships are similar to elements and relationships in the objects and events being denoted. It is a "natural" relationship. For example, a portrait looks like the person portrayed. In the digital code, the code elements are (a) discrete and (b) arbitrary. In other words, each code element is sharply different from others; the letter "a" is different from the letter "b," and the number "1" is distinct from the number "2." Second, the codes do not resemble the objects and events being denoted; their assignment is arbitrary. The letter "a" does not resemble an object in the real world. Or, the word "ape" does not resemble the active, furry creature we apply that label to.

Iconicity

Within the analogic codes, we find a range of *iconicity*. The *icon* bears a strong, clear resemblance to what is represented. The word "icon" was originally applied to carved, painted religious statues. But now it refers very broadly to any symbol which looks like its referent. Some symbols, of course, are more iconic than others; they bear a stronger resemblance. For example, a full-color motion picture of an individual has high "iconicity." A still, color photograph has less iconicity than the cinema but more iconicity than a black-and-white drawing (see Figure 4-1).

In the analogic codes, a variety of elements or relationships may be preserved or made iconic. Sometimes, three-dimensionality is preserved, as in a model. Sometimes color is preserved, as in film or a painting. But sometimes the underlying relationships are captured, as in a blueprint, map, or X-ray. Finally, the analogic code may present a very abstract symbol of the referent, a symbol which attempts to capture the feeling or movement or spirit; modern abstract art is in this category.

These three types of symbols have names: (a) *icons* are those which bear a strong outward appearance; (b) *schematics* are those which capture underlying relationships (e.g., a map is a "schematic"); and (c)

FIGURE 4-1 Iconicity: Digital and Analogic Coding.

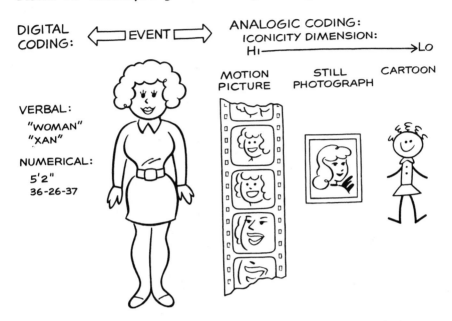

Digital codes have discrete code elements and formal rules for combining those elements; digital codes can name or quantify. Analogic codes bear some resemblance to the elements or relationships in the events they represent. They can range from high iconicity (with great similarity to the event) to low iconicity (with little similarity).

abstractions are those which, like modern art, capture the feeling or function of an object or event. In each type of symbol, however, we may find a range of "iconicity." For example, some maps are more iconic than others. And some abstract art is more representational, more iconic, than other art.

Consequences

When the communicator selects a coding strategy—either analogic or digital—it is likely to have consequences for the communication system. Typically, the digital codes take less effort for the communicator to encode—provided that he knows the code. Speaking takes less energy than acting or reenacting. Writing or typing usually takes less effort than making a painting or a motion picture or a three-dimensional model. For the receiver, however, the ratio may be reversed. It may be easier to look at a picture than to read a page of type.

The codes also differ in the learning they require. The digital code must be learned, since its relationships to referents are arbitrary. With the analogic codes, however, relatively little learning may be required. In general, the more iconic the symbol, the less prior learning required. The analogic symbol may require some learning, however. This is particularly true in the case of the schematic and the abstraction.

Many writers feel that the analogic symbol has more impact and that it is particularly effective in communicating certain types of information, for example spatial relationships. The receiver may indeed respond "more directly" to the analogic symbol, more like he would to the actual event. And spatial relationships may be easier to see on a map, for example, than when presented in a string of verbal directions.

We will want to return to this issue again in later chapters. But we can now turn from this general introduction to code systems and look more closely at the way man learns and uses his communication codes. In its broadest sense, the word "communication" comes from the same root as common, community, communion, commonality. It has to do with how men, who are different, become common: how they reach a community of meaning, a communion of understanding, a commonality of purpose. But scholars have long pondered just how that comes to be. How is it that one mind can affect another, using abstract signs which often have little or no apparent similarity to things being discussed?

HUMAN SIGN PROCESSES

Man is an active agent in the world. He produces his own energy. He directs it at his environment. He channels it toward goals of his own choosing. Moment by moment, he processes stimuli. He sorts. He sifts. He interprets. He infers. He manipulates his uncertainty and the uncertainty of others. And at the center of this activity is his use of signs. Signs and patterns of signs are produced, transmitted, interpreted, stored. Signs fuel interaction. Signs fire the imagination. Signs ignite man's potential for shared understanding.

Man, the Uncertainty Manipulator

In thinking about man as a communication receiver, it is easy to imagine him as a passive receptacle. For example, we might be tempted to think: a message stimulus comes in; and he reacts. If no message, no reaction. A more accurate picture of man sees him as active, aggressively seeking information, constantly exploring. While awake, he is in a continual state of tension. He maintains a plateau of uncertainty. He constructs expectations. He tests. He checks. He develops new predictions.

To understand man is to understand his use of information, not merely his use of matter or energy. Some human interactions do involve the direct transmission of energy. If I want you to sit down, I could shove you. Your change of state would come about via physical force. But man has learned that he can save a lot of energy by communicating. I can say, "Have a seat." Or I can smile and gesture to a chair. If you take a seat, you have provided the energy, not me. You have received, through light or sound, signals of very low energy. But they have been enough for you to interpret. They have reduced your uncertainty. You know what is expected. And you can act accordingly, if you wish.

As man moves through time and space he confronts a constantly shifting set of alternatives. His level of uncertainty at any moment depends on the number of alternatives in front of him. If he has a lot of alternatives, he is likely to have a lot of uncertainty. But his uncertainty also depends on the probabilities he sees among the alternatives. You know today that it will either rain or it will not rain. If the weather man tells you there is zero probability of rain, you have low uncertainty. You don't need to take a raincoat when you go out. If the weather man says there is a 100 percent chance of rain, you also don't have much uncertainty. But if he tells you there's a 50 percent probability of rain, your uncertainty is maximum. You don't know whether to take rainwear or not. You must begin to explore the likelihood of other alternatives. What is the chance that you'll actually get caught outside while it's raining? How uncomfortable would it be if you were? How does that possibility weigh against the nuisance of carrying rain gear?

Because man is a smart animal he has learned that he can reduce his uncertainty by observing certain stimuli. Some of the stimuli in his environment are especially useful because they help him predict other potential stimuli. In short, some stimuli "stand for" other stimuli. We can use them to make inferences about the not-here and not-now or about the yet-to-be. We call such stimuli *signs*.

Markers or Sign Vehicles

The physical stimulus itself, the pattern of matter or energy, is called a *marker* or, sometimes, a *sign vehicle*. (The term "marker" is used in systems theory and it is the one I prefer. Unfortunately, it can be a little confusing in nonverbal communication since the term "marker" has also been used to indicate a particular kind of gesture, one which marks off a portion of the communication.) The markers, as we are using the term here, is the observable event. The word on a page is a marker. So is the pattern of illumination on a television screen. So is the sound or movement produced by man.

If, for some receiver, these markers stand for something else, then—for that receiver—the marker is a *sign*. The word "cow," on a page, is a marker. If a receiver knows English, and if for that receiver the word "cow" stands for that four-legged critter grazing in the pasture, then, for that receiver, "cow" is a sign. Signs elicit meanings in the receiver. They can be interpreted. They are understood.

This means, of course, that the same marker may be a sign for one man and not for another. One man may look at the red spots on your face and say, "Look at the funny red spots." A doctor may look at the same markers and say, "Measles!" A wife may see her husband make movements, consciously or unconsciously, which indicate he's ready to leave the party. Others may see the same movements, but for them the markers are not a "sign" of anything. Similarly, the psychiatrist may make inferences on the basis of his patient's behavior. For the untrained observer, the same behaviors, the same markers, would be meaningless.

SIGNS: SIGNALS AND SYMBOLS

The examples given so far illustrate a number of different types of sign. But two major kinds are frequently observed: *signals* and *symbols*. Figure 4-2 diagrams the process of moving from event to marker to sign. It notes the two types of signs: signals and symbols. And it relates this to the coding strategies we learned earlier: the analogic, iconic, versus the digital, arbitrary.

Signals

Signals are distinguished from symbols largely on the basis of their function in communication systems. A signal is a type of sign which is likely to trigger action or expectations from the receiver. The word "Go!" is a signal to start activity. Similarly, the green traffic light is a signal to start moving.

Signals are frequently the heralds of other events. The traffic light warns us that cars are going to start moving, or stop moving, and we can take appropriate action. In this case, the signal tells us about events outside the communication system. In terms of our ABX-X′ model, the signal is an X′ talking about some X in the environment.

But signals can also operate within the communication system. They can be the small signals from A to B that "Now it's your turn to talk." Or,

FIGURE 4-2 Human Sign Processes.

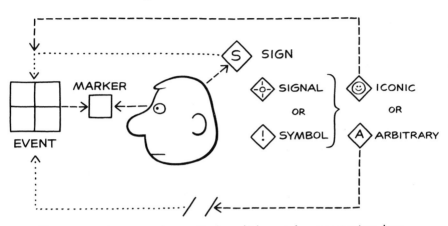

The event produces a marker; a stimulus, which may, for some receiver, have sign value. It may be a signal or a symbol. In either case, it may be iconic or arbitrary. Signs, in turn, appear in larger sign patterns.

"Now I have something to say." This may be done with a glance, a head nod, a smile, or a hand gesture. Similarly, signals operate within the code system: they are code elements which warn us that other code elements are coming. In one sense, the word "the" is a signal that a noun is approaching. A period signals the end of a sentence. An indentation signals the start of a paragraph.

Signals can be further distinguished by the way they relate to the events they herald. A *symptom*, for instance, signals some state, such as illness. The red spots are a symptom of measles. The coding is "natural" rather than "arbitrary." An *index* is another type of signal which points to some other event, usually one in close spatial or temporal relationship. The large headline indexes an important news story; the smaller headline indexes a less important news story. A red light signals the left side of a ship, or the left wing of an airplane; it is an index of left from right.

Symbols

Symbols are those signs which are not signals; they are the pictures and words and marks and sounds which stand for other objects and events. They elicit meanings from the receiver, denotative meanings and connotative meanings. But they do not demand action; they only ask to be interpreted. They do not herald the arrival of other events. They can talk about the not-here and the not-now, events which may be far removed in time and space.

Both signals and symbols can be encoded either analogically or digitally. The word "Go!" is a digital signal. It is coded arbitrarily; in another language it would be another term. To some extent, the green and red traffic lights are also arbitrary. Other color coding could have been used: for example, purple and orange or pink and blue. An example of an iconic signal is the shadow of a chicken hawk; this pattern (which is analogic to the configuration of the hawk) will send a duckling into hiding.

The analogic–digital distinction may, however, become most important with the symbol. It is in presenting—or re-presenting—the not-here and the not-now that the analogic symbol may be most powerful. Similarly, it is in the digital symbol that we see the amazing efficiency of the human sign process. Man can store, transmit, receive, and retrieve vast stores of knowledge by manipulating 26 letters and 10 numbers.

Sign Patterns

As we use the term "sign" in this book it may apply to a single stimulus or a whole pattern of stimulation. Like our use of the term "system," we will apply "sign" to the symbolic level we are examining. But at times the "sign" will have many subsystems, other signs which go to make up the larger symbol. For example, we might take the picture of a face as a sign. But within this symbol, the line representing the mouth is also a sign.

Occasionally, we will want to draw attention to the fact that we are talking about a configuration of signs, and in those instances we will use the term *sign pattern*. In short, a sign pattern is a system made up of other signs. And in this pattern, as in any system, the relationships are likely to be important. The total facial expression may be a sign pattern. So would be a picture layout, or a movie sequence.

This may help us over a point of frequent confusion in nonverbal communication. Often, we think of signs as specific stimuli which elicit responses (e.g., denotative and connotative meanings). But when we begin to examine communication systems in operation we quickly note the importance of pattern. Man, as an active communicator, frames expectations. And he acts on them. He doesn't merely wait for meaningful stimuli to arrive.

As a result, when an expected sign does *not* occur, *that* is meaningful, too. When you smilingly say, "Good morning," to a friend and he does not respond, you wonder what is wrong. If you think of signs as only the presentation of specific stimuli, you will have trouble analyzing that situation. It appears that you are reacting to a nonsign, or the lack of a sign.

If, however, you recognize the larger system of signs, the sign pattern, your friend's nonresponse is part of an important event which may well signal that something is amiss.

CODES: VERBAL AND NONVERBAL

In verbal language we find an extremely complex code system, with numerous elements, many rules for organizing those elements, and a vast number of rules for relating elements to referents. There are 26 letters in the alphabet. They can be combined, by complex rules, into a vast number of words. Using other rules, these words can, in turn, be combined into an infinite set of sentences. We have called these rules of code organization: syntactic rules. Finally, other rules—semantic rules—relate these words and patterns to events outside the code system. Using words, man can encode his loftiest ideals, his most profound thoughts. He can speak of the distant past, the far reaches of the universe, the events which exist only in man's imagination.

Language is subtle and complex in ways that are not immediately obvious. For example, part of its power and efficiency arises from using many levels of organization. At the basic level are relatively few elements, 26 letters of the alphabet, or some 47 distinct sounds or "phonemes." But these basic elements are not assigned meanings via the semantic rules. (We can use "A" to mean a grade, and the letter "a" is also *a* word; but most words require several sounds.)

Meaning enters at the word level, or at what the linguist calls the "morpheme" level. By changing the order of our basic elements we can completely change the meaning. The word "pin" is different from the reverse order of letters—"nip." By easy-to-produce substitutions, we can also change meaning. The word "pin" is totally different from "bin," although only one small sound has been changed. Using a handful of basic code elements we can order and reorder to generate a vast vocabulary of usable symbols.

Similarly, ordering allows us to expand our meaning universe at the sentence level. Earlier, we gave the example of "The boy downed the beer" versus "The beer downed the boy." Ordering and reordering our vocabulary of word symbols we can express an ever-widening circle of ideas.

Linguistics, the systematic study of language, is several centuries old. We now know a great deal about the structure of language around the world. In spite of this long history of study, however, many mysteries remain. New theories emerge. Old notions are overturned. Very recently, the theories of Noam Chomsky have had a major impact on the way linguists view language. But because we do know so much about spoken language, it is tempting to apply the same theories, the same methodologies, when we try to "break another code," the code of the nonverbal. If it works, we have profited from the centuries of painstaking work in linguistics.

Kinesics

The most ambitious attempt to apply the linguistic model is in an area known as *kinesics*, the study of body movement.[1] The pioneer in the field is Ray L. Birdwhistell, a scholar trained in anthropology and linguistics. Birdwhistell, especially in his early writings, argued that "body language" may be similar to "spoken language." Movements have communication value. They are learned within a culture, like language. And they have a complex, multilevel structure like language. Finally, he argued, the methodologies which have served the linguist so well should be useful in tackling this new problem.

Spoken language is built up of rudimentary sounds, *phones*, which are lumped into the crucial speech sounds, the *phonemes*. These in turn are organized into *morphemes*, or word-like units. In body movement, Birdwhistell called the rudimentary movement a *kine*. These may be interchangeable within a unit known as the *kineme*, which in turn is combined into larger units such as the *kinemorph*.

The human voice can, of course, make thousands of possible sounds which might be discriminated by a hearer. However, only about two dozen sounds are sorted out for use as the basic building blocks of speech—the phonemes. In each language, the number of these key sounds is small, usually under one hundred. The sounds which are selected may vary from language to language. But each language has its small repertoire of important sound elements.

In producing one of these key sound elements, there is, of course, great variation. One person's pronunciation of "a" is slightly different from someone else's production of "a." Even the same person's enunciation of a sound differs over time. It may not be the same when he is tired, or in a hurry, or excited. In decoding language, we, of course, overlook these differences. We lump similar sounds together. The discriminable differences, or phones, are ignored as we attend to the important speech categories, the phonemes. In the linguist's terminology, interchangeable phones are called *allophones* of the same phoneme. In

[1] Ray L. Birdwhistell, *Kinesics and Context* (Philadelphia: University of Pennsylvania Press, 1970).

some languages, for example, the "p" and "b" sounds are allophones of a common phoneme, whereas in English they distinguish two different phonemes.

Birdwhistell has applied this same principle to the analysis of movement. As we watch someone move, we can discriminate thousands of movements. These basic discriminations would be called *kines*. But only some of these kines really make a difference. Many are *allokines* of the same *kineme*. To take an example, a high-speed camera might reveal several hundred discriminable positions in the closing of an eyelid. Birdwhistell argues, however, that in normal viewing we only discriminate eleven positions, or kines. But even these eleven are not all "meaningful." We usually lump these 11 into six important categories, what Birdwhistell would label kinemes. The six he sees as being important for communication are (a) open-eyed, (b) droopy-lidded, (c) squinting, (d) eyes squeezed tight, (e) just open, and (f) closed.

At the next highest level, the linguist is interested in how sounds (phonemes) combine into word-like structures, or "morphemes." Again, the analysis is similar. There are some combinations, or "morphs," which are discriminably different from others. But they may turn out to be interchangeable, or "allomorphs" within a single morpheme. By analogy, Birdwhistell would look for the combinations of basic movements into meaningful *kinemorphs*. The closed eye, by itself, might not elicit any particular meaning. But combined with a furrowed brow and a downturned mouth, it would become part of a word-like configuration meaning: sadness. On the other hand, a closed eye combined with a yawning mouth might have a different meaning: fatigue.

Moving to a higher level, the linguist examines the word in phrases and in sentences and finally moves to the utterance in its total context. The kinesic researcher similarly moves to total acts, to actions involving several acts, and finally to the action in its larger context. While we have traced the kinesic approach starting with the smallest unit, the kinesic methodology actually moves in the other direction. Birdwhistell and his associates start with the action in context and he argues that the individual kinemorph cannot be understood unless it is seen against this larger backdrop. He warns against the notion of a dictionary of kinemorphs which tell you: when you see such a movement, it means this.

Other Nonverbal "Languages"

The linguistic model can, of course, be applied to other nonverbal codes. Figure 4-3 outlines a terminology for each of the major codes that can be produced by a fundamental motor act. Developed initially by Martin Krampen, this scheme has been elaborated by other researchers, among them James McCroskey. In particular, Edward T. Hall, an anthropologist, has suggested that all of culture can be analyzed into "primary message systems."[2] He sees communication in man's use of time and space, his work and play activities, in learning, defense, sexuality. In each area of life, Hall sees these messages structured very much like language. He identifies what he calls *isolates*, *sets*, and *patterns*, concepts that are comparable to phonemes, morphemes, and syntax in spoken language. In a similar vein, the linguist Kenneth Pike has suggested that man's behavior can be analyzed linguistically and he has proposed the term *behavioreme*.

Of the dozen areas outlined in Figure 4-3, only a couple have received intensive exploration. Birdwhistell, Albert Scheflen, and other researchers have elaborated the kinesic approach.[3] And researchers such as Edward Hall and Michael Watson have pursued the proxemic approach.[4]

Differences

Kinesics and proxemics are still youthful areas of study—under 30 years of age. For that reason it is still difficult to assess their eventual worth. But it seems increasingly clear that the linguistic model has some

FIGURE 4-3 Possible Human Code Systems.

Fundamental motor act	Basic unit produced	Combined into	Studied by	Typical act or skill
uttering	phoneme	morpheme	linguistics	poetry
scratching }	glyph	glytomorph	glyptics	writing
	pict	pictomorph	pictics	drawing
molding	plasm	plastomorph	plastics	sculpture
building	technem	technomorph	tectonics	architecture
moving	kine	kinemorph	kinesics	dance
sound	tone	melos	melodics	music
touch	hapton	haptomorph	haptics	fondling
produce smell	ozone	aroma	aromatics	perfumery
produce taste	edon	edomorph	edetics	cooking
space arrangement	proxeme	proxemorph	proxemics	city planning
time arrangement	chron	chronomorph	chronemics	timing
filming	edeme	edemorph	vidistics	cinema

[2] Edward T. Hall, *The Silent Language* (Greenwich, Conn.: Fawcett, 1959).
[3] Albert E. Scheflen, *Body Language and the Social Order* (Englewood Cliffs, N.J.: Prentice-Hall, 1972).
[4] Michael Watson, *Proxemic Behavior: A Cross-Cultural Study* (The Hague: Mouton, 1970).

difficulties, when applied across the board to nonverbal behavior. There may be important differences between verbal and nonverbal code systems.

1. Not all nonverbal codes share the complex, multilevel structure of language. In particular, it is often difficult to find the counterpart of the phone or the phoneme, discrete elements which do not have meaning in themselves but which can be combined in various ways to produce other meaningful symbols. Similarly, jumping a level, many nonverbal codes do not seem to have the complex rules of syntax which in verbal language produce the sentence.

2. The nature of the code element, the basic marker, may be different. In particular, the verbal elements are perceived as "discrete" while many nonverbal elements seem "continuous." The letter "a" is distinctly different from the letter "b." But colors, or lines, or movements seem to flow into each other. There are no obvious steps from one to another. This, in turn, means that nonverbal researchers are still trying to find appropriate "units of analysis," a problem largely solved for the linguist.

3. Many nonverbal codes are iconic rather than arbitrary. The relationship between the nonverbal code element and its referent is often "natural" in that there is some kind of resemblance. Meanwhile in language, sign-to-referent associations are arbitrary and learned.

4. In this vein, not all nonverbal signs are learned in the same way as language. There is now evidence, for example, that the facial expressions associated with certain basic emotions are panhuman (i.e., they are found in men around the world). To the extent that facial expressions are automatic and involuntary, they are "symptoms" rather than learned "symbols." This, of course, presents a different problem for analysis than the one typically faced by the linguist.

5. Finally, the traditional methodologies which have proved so fruitful in linguistics may be less appropriate for many nonverbal codes. In traditional linguistic analysis, the linguist found an informant who knew the language. He then asked him to produce sounds, and the linguist in turn tried out hypotheses. He might ask, for example, if there was a difference between "pin" and "bin." If so, the linguist would know that the small difference between the sounds of "p" and "b" makes a big difference in that language. The linguist did not worry about sampling informants, since everyone in the culture would know the common language. And the linguist assumed, rightly, that his informant could produce the important differences and recognize them when someone else produced them.

But with the kinesic informant, difficulties arise. For example, the speaker gets feedback both from the movements of his mouth and from the sound he hears. He knows when he's made a "slip of the tongue," not because he feels it in his tongue, but because he hears the sound he has produced. But the kinesic informant only gets internal feedback. He knows how the move feels. But he doesn't see how the facial expression or movement looks to another. He may not detect his "slips of the face." As a result, the kinesic informant may have difficulty producing the "same" movement twice. He knows there's "something there" but he is unreliable as a producing informant.

In summary, the linguistic tradition offers a potentially powerful model for examining nonverbal codes. There are, however, important differences between many nonverbal codes and man's complex, multileveled, spoken language. Increasingly, it appears that the kinesic approach is going to be most useful in areas closely related to language. Some movements, for example, seem to be interchangeable with vocal paralinguistic events. Instead of a pause or a stress, the speaker may substitute a minor body movement. And, certain movements of the head, eye, and hand appear at predictable points in linguistic discourse. For analyzing these events, a grasp of the linguistic model may be especially important.

NONVERBAL CODE SYSTEMS

If we do not expect all nonverbal codes to resemble the complex structure of spoken language, what other approaches might be taken to organize the codes for analysis? The simplest is merely to group the code systems by the way in which the markers are produced. Two basic systems would be *performance codes* and *artifactual codes*. In addition, two derived codes would seem to exhaust the range of man-made markers; the *spatiotemporal codes* and the *mediatory codes* (Figure 4-4).

The *performance codes* are those produced by direct actions of a human communicator using his own body. Included are facial expressions, eye behavior, head nods, posture, hand gestures, and body movements. Also included are the noises which can be made by a human actor: humming, laughing, grunting, yawning, snapping the fingers, clapping, and so on. In addition, man can touch. He can transmit body heat. He can produce odors. He can even produce tastes. (Licking is part of social interaction for many animals. It is less so in humans, but kissing may transmit taste, and for an infant the taste of mother's milk may be an important part of a significant early interaction.)

For the receiver, the performance codes are taken in through all the senses. He sees the facial expressions and body movements. He hears the vocalizations and other sounds. He feels the touch and heat. He smells odors and he tastes tastes. This means, of course, that the receiver can have a simultaneous flow of signs in many sense modalities. Similarly,

Figure 4-4 Major Nonverbal Codes.

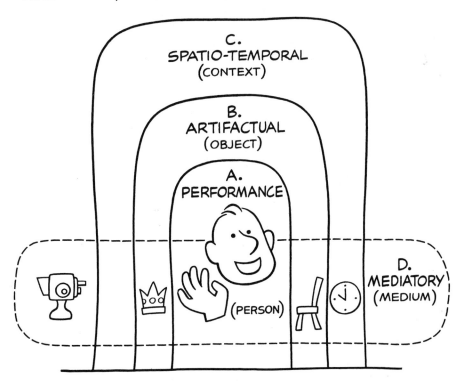

The human communicator has several codes at his command, including (A) performance, arising out of the use of the body; (B) artifactual, employing objects; (C) spatio-temporal, arising in the use of time and space; and (D) mediatory, emerging in the use of media.

the sender can transmit an array of performance code markers all at the same time.

Artifactual codes are produced with objects; they are the signs that arise when artifacts are produced, arranged, displayed, or presented by a human. Code elements may involve objects that an individual carries: cosmetics, jewelry, clothing, handbags, badges, insignia, and individual tools and properties such as pencils, pipes, and glasses. Larger artifactual codes include chairs, tables, art objects, and tools and equipment, such as typewriters, cars, and motorboats. Finally, the artifactual codes may include large, relatively immobile objects such as public monuments, homes, and other architectural structures.

For the receiver, most artifactual markers are seen. But they can be heard: car horns, timers, bell buoys, cow bells. They can be felt: pillows, chairs, clothing texture, hot coffee, cold beer. They can be smelled: perfume, fresh baking, old gyms. They can be tasted: wine, cheese, cigars. The receiver can simultaneously attend to several artifactual signs.

⌈ *Spatio-temporal codes* are created through the arrangement and use of time and space. They arise out of the performance and artifacts of a communicator. But they bear singling out for special attention. Time and space form the backdrop for all communication situations. They are the context within which all communication takes place. For that reason we usually do not think of time and space as something which can be manipulated as a message element. But particularly as we move across cultures, we find that people have different ways of cutting up time and space. When others do not cut up these vital dimensions in the same way, this is noted as a message with distinct meaning. ⌉

Mediatory codes are created through invention, selection, arrangement, and presentation within a medium. They appear within a particular type of human artifact: photographs, films, videotapes, graphs, charts, cartoons, statues, recordings, publications, and so on. Within each medium, the communicator has options. He can arrange and rearrange. He can change size and color. He can change volume and sound effect. He can reorder time and space. For the professional communicator, this opens up new vistas of entertainment and education, persuasion and manipulation.

In summary, the markers of the nonverbal domain can be grouped into four code systems according to the way they are produced. In succeeding chapters we will ask additional questions. Can they also be grouped according to their function in the communication process? Do they differ in origin, in the way they enter man's sign repertoire? Do they code different kinds of content? And in different ways? Are some more effective and efficient than others? With our initial grouping, however, we can begin to explore the use of nonverbal code systems.

DISCUSSION–EXERCISES

1. Review the concepts at the beginning of this chapter. How many do you feel you understand now? For how many could you present a *nonverbal* illustration?

2. From what you have learned about code systems in this chapter, compare arabic numbers (1, 2, 3, etc.) and Roman numerals (I, II, III, etc.). What are the basic code elements? What are the rules of syntax? What are the semantic rules? Are they digital or analogic? Is one easier

to learn than the other? Is one easier to use (e.g., for addition or sub-traction)?

3. Analyze the face of a clock as a code system. Is it analogic? Or digital? What are the rules of syntax? The semantic rules?

4. Take a photograph or cartoon and try to analyze it the way a linguist would analyze language. What would be the counterpart of a sentence? A morpheme? A phoneme?

5. Examine the "Right"–"Right" cartoon and try to identify performance, artifactual, spatio-temporal, and mediatory codes. Can you find examples of each?

5

systems for prediction

This chapter is designed to

1. Introduce you to four levels of prediction for communication behavior:
   - physiological
   - psychological
   - social
   - cultural

2. Examine the explanatory power of these levels with three types of communication behavior:
   - encoding
   - processing
   - decoding

3. Encourage you to examine the roots of your own communication behavior.

4. Stimulate you to think about the predictions you make about the communication behavior of others.

THOUGHT STARTERS

1. How well can you predict the communication behaviors of others?

2. How do you do it?

"I don't think so," Bill says finally.

"I don't understand you," Al says, an annoyed frown flickering across his brow. "You're a virile, young male. You've got a good personality. You have fun when you're with people. It's not un-American to go out with girls, you know."

"All right. I'll do it."

AL SAYS HE DOESN'T UNDERSTAND HIS ROOMMATE. But he's touched all the bases: the physiological level, the psychological, the social, and the cultural. He's probed each level of possible prediction and explanation. Somewhere, in one of these frames, he seems to have hit his mark.

In man's attempt to understand himself, and in his attempt to predict the communication behavior of others, he uses a multileveled frame of explanation. He knows that he, and his fellow men, are shaped by the systems to which they belong. If he knows the other communicator is human, he can make certain predictions. If he knows which culture the communicator grew up in, he can make a more refined set of predictions. If he knows something about the communicator's social roles, or about his personality, the predictions can be honed even more. This chapter examines three types of communication behavior: the encoding, processing, and decoding of nonverbal cues. It lays them against four levels of prediction: the physiological, the psychological, the social, and the cultural.

Figure 5-1 presents a model of man's communication behavior in terms of levels of prediction and explanation. In the outer frame are the cultural constraints or determinants of man's behavior. These factors are studied in anthropology. They tell us what all members of a culture will have learned, will think is appropriate, will perform in given cultural contexts. The next frame points to social constraints, the behaviors man will perform in a group. The fact that a human being is in a particular role—

FIGURE 5-1   Levels of Prediction for Communication Behavior.

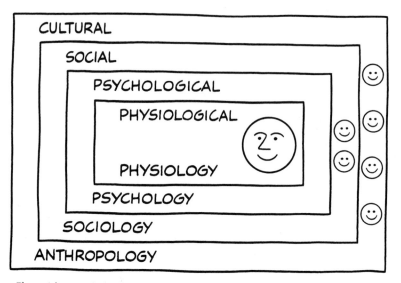

The prediction of man's communication activity may require knowledge about the physiological, psychological, social, and cultural systems which shape and constrain his behavior.

father, mother, husband, sister, student—means that certain behaviors are more likely than others. The next frame focuses on psychological factors, the behaviors arising out of individual personality systems, out of beliefs and values and attitudes held by an individual. Finally, in the most inner frame, are the physical constraints. Some are panhuman (i.e., they are found universally among human beings). All normal men have eyes and ears and limbs that bend in certain ways. There are, of course, great individual differences in the acuity of senses, in strength, capacity, and so on. But these basic physical factors also help explain what cues man will produce, what signs are likely to arise.

THE PHYSIOLOGICAL SYSTEM

The human animal can receive nonverbal signs through the sense of sight, through hearing, smelling, tasting, and touching. Unlike the lower animals, man has an enormous capacity to process the signs he receives. He can make complex inferences on the basis of subtle cues. He can store memories of past events. He can conjure up images of events which will happen in the future—or which can never happen. Finally, man can produce signs with great ease. He can spin out a range of symbols which become available for other humans to interpret.

Decoding

Of man's sensory receptors, the eye is the most powerful. It can make more discriminations. It has the farthest range (i.e., we can see great distances, all the way to the stars). The ear is perhaps the next most powerful receptor. It permits an impressive range of discriminations, and it allows us to hear events which take place up to a few hundred feet away. The sense of smell is in the near range. A surprising number of odors can be discriminated. But the source of the odor usually has to be fairly close to the nose. The skin is a more versatile receptor than is sometimes realized. It is also man's largest sense organ. It is sensitive to pressure as in touch. But it also picks up heat; it is a thermal receptor. This means that stimuli must be close, and either much hotter or colder than skin temperature. Or the stimuli must actually touch the skin, creating pressure. Finally, the sense of taste is perhaps the most intimate receptor, taking place within the oral cavity. Again, however, a surprising number of stimuli can be discriminated in terms of sweet and sour, hot and cold, and so on.

This array of senses differs from the distribution found in lower animals and insects. In the insect world, chemical communication is primary. Insects leave trails of chemicals and follow trails left by others. Similarly, in most of the animal kingdom, the sense of smell plays an important role. While other creatures surpass the human in one or more sensory dimensions, man has a range which provides an enormous variety of inputs. Perhaps even more importantly, he can process these sensory inputs and make inferences in a way which is unknown elsewhere in the animal world.

In responding to his sensory inputs, man structures his perceptions in what might be called a natural grammar of nonverbal cues. Items which are seen together in time and space tend to be seen as related. Similarly, items which are similar in some aspect—color, shape, size, and so on—tend to be grouped together. Finally, elements that share common movement tend to be seen as a group. Conversely, items which are in sharp contrast, in color, shape, or texture, tend to be seen as different. Usually, man's perception is selective and some elements of the environment become "figure" standing out from "ground." In turn, the elements which are identified as figure get much more careful attention. These are some of the "Gestalt" principles which have attempted to account for the way man makes sense out of the myriad inputs which impinge on his sensory receptors.

Processing

A long-standing argument in psychology has to do with the extent to which man can "think" nonverbally. One school argues that all perceptions are processed verbally and that we think in words. Another school argues that this may happen with some stimuli, but that other perceptions are processed without the benefit of verbal mediators. We can, in short, engage in nonverbal mental imagery. These two models are illustrated in Figure 5-2.

In Figure 5-2a, stimulus events, verbal or nonverbal, are perceived and then processed via verbal mediators leading to a verbal or nonverbal response. Figure 5-2b sketches an alternative, in which stimulus events are perceived but then processed either via verbal mediators or via nonverbal imagery.

Recent research on brain physiology indicates that the two hemispheres of the brain may function somewhat differently in the processing of information. The left hemisphere appears particularly adept at handling verbal, temporal, and digital material. Meanwhile, the right hemisphere tends to handle the nonverbal, the spatial, and analogic.

Additional recent research on the brain builds on the analogy of the

FIGURE 5-2   Patterns of Mental Mediation.

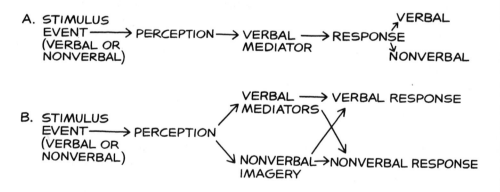

A. One model of information processing suggests that stimuli are funneled through verbal mediators.
B. An alternative model suggests that mental processing includes both verbal mediators and nonverbal imagery.

hologram. Holography, of course, is a new technology which, using laser beams, can produce three-dimensional reproductions of reality. The startling thing about holography is that from the smallest segment of a holographic plate the whole picture can be reproduced. With more of the plate, the picture becomes stronger, but it is intact even with the smallest segment. This, in turn, appears to be how certain aspects of the brain work. Memory is not stored in various pigeonholes and retrieved by verbal tags. Rather, information appears to be stored in much the way it is on a holographic plate. This, in turn, means that the language of the brain is probably quite different than the verbal language men use between themselves.

While new research is turning up exciting leads about man's cognitive patterns, other research is probing man's affective states. This work on man's emotions appears especially important in nonverbal communication since some traditional cues, namely facial expressions, figure importantly in these theories. Other nonverbal cues, such as color, movement, complexity of pattern, and sound, appear to be related to arousal. Given the right cues, man is more attentive, more alert, better able to receive and process information.

Encoding

Different physiological states lead to different nonverbal cues and behaviors. These in turn may become signals for an observer trying to diagnose the states of the individual. Eye movements and pupil dilation are related to attention. Tension and exertion lead to perspiration, and this in turn leads to odor—and a multimillion dollar industry aimed at disguising that signal. Some internal states lead to changes in the amount of blood in the surface tissue of the skin. Individuals blush or blanche. Excitation leads to a change in the speed of body movements. And emotions are reflected in the muscle contractions of the face.

In addition to these basic physiological responses, men the world over exhibit patterns of expression. What is expressed and the way it is expressed differs. But the expression itself takes place. In most societies, for instance, men make music and dance. Most societies exhibit some form of drawing and the artistic decoration of artifacts. In most areas of the world, humans wear at least some form of clothing, and typically this costume has a decorative as well as a practical function.

In muscle, mind, and nerve, in sensory receptors and in organs of expression, man is graciously endowed with communication equipment. Spoken language appears to be a human universal. But so, too, is the production of a large range of nonverbal signs.

THE PSYCHOLOGICAL SYSTEM

The physiological spectrum presents a range of alternatives in decoding, processing, and encoding. Some men are stronger or more sensitive or more talented. And these individuals may become our outstanding nonverbal communicators, the famous artists, dancers, and musicians. But even within the "normal" range of physiological possibilities, most of us don't use all the possibilities. Individual personalities, values, needs, attitudes, and beliefs lead us to use part of the spectrum and not other parts. As individuals we sharpen some of our attributes. And we let others fall into disuse.

Decoding

Although all men are selective in their perceptions, just what they will select is shaped by psychological forces. What will be "figure" for one man will be unimportant "ground" for another. The man with a high need to dominate might, for example, be very sensitive to cues of submission in other people. The man or woman with a strong sex drive is going to be tuned in (and turned on) by another type of cue.

Through learning, some individuals appear to develop a preference for one modality over another. Some prefer to see a message while others would rather hear it. Some people rely on their sense of touch while others avoid tactile stimuli. Children, of course, put everything in their mouths, to see how it tastes, to see how it feels. Later in life we tend to be more careful what we sample with our taste buds.

Some individuals may be quite sensitive to a type of nonverbal cue that others hardly notice. Some women, for example, are very fashion conscious. They note and remember what other women wear. They make elaborate inferences about the other woman's taste, background, status, and sexual proclivities. Men may be aware vaguely of the latter, but they may be quite oblivious to the fashion items which made one woman seem "sexy" and another not so sexy. Similarly, some people seem more sensitive generally to facial expressions and the feelings of others. Some individuals can read maps and charts and graphs with ease. Others, for some reason, find them a life-long mystery.

Individual differences in decoding abilities are, of course, most noticeable with people suffering from severe personality disturbance. The emotionally disturbed person may "block" on the recognition of threatening facial expressions. The same blocking can be seen, to a lesser extent, in the normal population. Some individuals have difficulty recognizing anger, or fear, or disgust. Others may be particularly sensitive to these negative expressions.

Processing

Scientists have long suspected that individuals differ in their ability to process different types of information. In our culture, we tend to equate intelligence with the ability to process verbal and digital symbols (e.g., words and numbers). But obviously some geniuses may be inarticulate and nonmathematical yet able to excel in art or music. We may, in fact, have unrecognized "geniuses" in the areas of taste and smell. (Perhaps they become our famous chefs and perfume makers.)

Famous Sir Francis Bacon stumbled on one difference quite by accident. He was interested in how fellow scientists solved creative problems. He wrote friends asking just what they visualized when they worked on certain problems. But some of his friends were dumbfounded. They thought Sir Francis was getting mellow in the head—because they didn't visualize *anything*. Surprised, Sir Francis decided there must be "visualizers" and "verbalizers." Figure 5-3 shows how some people visualize the year. Some individuals have very clear impressions of what a year looks like, whereas other people have no imagery whatever.

In recent times scientists have thought that the difference in brain hemispheres might explain "visualizers" and "verbalizers." An early hypothesis was that one side became dominant while the other hemisphere was "underdeveloped." Recent evidence seems to indicate a more complex relationship. Apparently, people who are good at solving verbal problems are able to inhibit the activity of the right (or nonverbal) hemisphere while engaged in the verbal task. Similarly, good ability with nonverbal puzzles seems to require inhibition of the competing verbal hemisphere. At least part of the talent in one mode seems to come from the ability to eliminate "noise," or interference, from the other mode.

A practical implication for the communicator is: everyone may not be like you. It's tempting to think that because you learn easily with pictures—or with words—that other people will respond the same way. But that may not be the case.

Encoding

Some people always "talk with their hands." Others seldom gesture. As we will see, these differences can arise from culture, from ethnic group, from family. But part of the difference stems from personality. Some individuals are extroverted and flamboyant. Others are introverted and inhibited. Some people use particular kinds of gestures but not others.

FIGURE 5-3   Images of the Year.

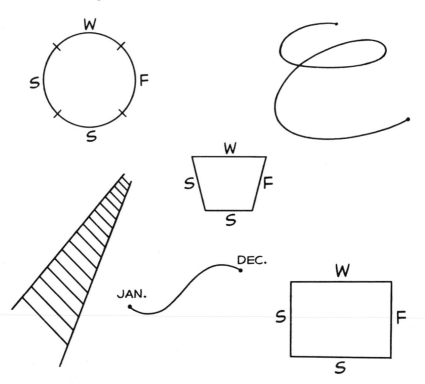

Some individuals have very clear visual images of abstract concepts such as the year. Even two "visualizers" who agree the year looks like a square may disagree sharply whether winter is on top or bottom—or on one side.

Some individuals have distinctive mannerisms which become a personal nonverbal signature. Sometimes these gestures are imitated in jest. At other times they can be quite infectious and diffuse through a group of friends without much awareness.

In some people the face reflects every nuance of inner feeling. Others might be named The Great Stone Face. Their poker-faced expression reveals nothing of their inner turmoil. Some people are very expressive with certain affects but do not display others. An individual may show happiness but inhibit his display of anger. Other grouches may inhibit happiness, but specialize in contempt, disgust, or anger.

Finally, personality differences may emerge in the art an individual produces, in his selection of clothing and decoration, in his use of time and space. Viktor Lowenfeld distinguished two kinds of artists, which he labeled "optics" and "haptics." The production of the "optic" has a strong visual sense. Meanwhile, the art of the "haptic" has a strong tactile quality. One gets a sense of closeness, of textures and shapes, of the way things would feel. Some individuals take a similar approach to clothing. Some are very concerned about how their costume looks. Meanwhile, others are oblivious to matters of style as long as the clothing feels good, as long as it is comfortable. (And then there are us skinflints who don't care how it looks or feels as long as it doesn't cost too much.)

THE SOCIAL SYSTEM

Man behaves differently when not alone. He suddenly must maintain a presentation of self. And some behaviors which one might do in private are not appropriate for public consumption. In addition, man must relate to others. He needs to affiliate with them, or fend them off. He needs to control, or be controlled. He needs to give affection, or he needs to get affection. Each desire requires the production of certain cues—and a response to the nonverbal signals of others.

In addition, man's behavior is shaped by the particular group he is in. He acts differently in church and in his favorite saloon. He exhibits a different latitude of behavior in the warmth of his family or the cold business world. Further, his actions will be molded to the particular role he plays in each group. Within the family, the father has a range of behaviors not permitted the son. The older brother may have different responsibilities from a younger brother, or from a son-in-law. Similarly, in the business world, the behaviors exhibited by the boss may not be appropriate for the employee.

Decoding

Within the social sphere, perceptual selectivity also screens the cues man uses. Where at the psychological level, this selectivity related to individual differences, on the social level this selectivity stems from roles and group norms. Two managers, although very different in personality, might be attuned to the same nonverbal cues—because of their executive role. Similarly, members of a group may be acutely aware of cues that others would miss. Initiates of a teenage gang might see sharp differences between themselves and others, in dress, hair style, ornaments, manners. Meanwhile, to the adult "all the kids look the same."

In the orchestration of social groups, three types of cues must be decoded with some accuracy. The first answers the question: Who is in and who is out? We must be able to tell "them" from "us." Sometimes groups have "gatekeepers" and "bouncers" to screen those wanting in and to eject those needing out. Often this sifting is done on the basis of nonverbal cues. We sort the "long-hairs" from the "fuzz," the "hard-hats" from the "eggheads," the "tenderfoot" from the "redneck," the "blue collar worker" from the "white collar worker." In less formal groupings, the question becomes: Who is available for interaction? How responsive are these people to being in my communication system? Again, nonverbal cues are crucial indicators. She turns toward him. He catches her gaze. She smiles. He leans toward her. She extends her hand. . . .

A second major problem is: Who's in charge here? To know how the group operates, to effectively influence its outcome, we need to know the power structure. We need to know who controls what. Here cues of status and influence become salient. Sometimes, it's easy. The guy with the gavel is the "head cheese." At other times, it's more difficult. The inconspicuous guy at the end of the table gives the nod which everybody follows. The reading of status cues is a popular game. Each year, the Kremlin watchers redraw the Soviet hierarchy on the basis of who stood where at the May Day parade. ·And as Shepard Mead illustrates in *How to Succeed in Business Without Really Trying,* cue catching—and casting —is a vital art for the aspiring young executive.

Finally, we need to know: Is everybody happy? For a group to operate smoothly, morale must be maintained. Strong negative emotions are likely to cause trouble. If extreme enough, they'll blow the group to smithereens. One role, the "socioemotional leader," is likely to bear special responsibility. He (or she) needs to sense the danger cues. Appropriate action must be taken, to soothe ruffled feathers, to dispel tensions with a bit of humor, to get the group back in harmony. Frequently, all members of the group share some responsibility. If one member is troublesome, several and perhaps all the members will give him cues. If he can't decode the signals—or refuses to—the cues will get stronger. Until finally the troublemaker is ejected from the group, usually with a set of cues that are hard to miss.

Processing

In social structures, certain individuals and certain groups are charged with processing information. They gather, sift, store, retrieve, and disseminate. The journalist gathers and distributes the news of the day. The advertising firm and the public relations firm process and inject the information which best represents the client. Educators gather and regurgitate information which they think will interest students. Libraries gather and distribute more information, acting as the memory banks of society.

At a less formal level, each of us plays the role of information processor for some group. We gather and filter (and sometimes elaborate) information for our friendship circle, a process sometimes known as "gossip." We may be charged with gathering information and making a report, for our fellow students, for our business colleagues. We may be asked to keep the minutes of the meeting. And if we stay in a group long enough we may emerge as the informal historian who can tell how it was "way back when."

While serving in these processor roles, we use nonverbal cues in a number of ways. We may use nonverbal cues to screen our sources. Some are more knowledgeable. Some are more reliable. We may examine cues in the information itself. Is it internally consistent? Are there any cues which suggest it might be "manufactured" or unauthentic? We may use other cues for storage and retrieval: color coding, format, location. Finally, we may attend to important cues when we present our information. A cable may get more attention than a letter. We may have to use the appropriate format: stationery instead of scratch paper, a typewriter instead of a pencil. Authenticity may require seals and signatures. Timeliness may demand a typewritten page rather than printed text.

Finally, the organizational channels of information processing are frequently traced with nonverbal signs. Some are classic stereotypes, such as the reporter with a press card in his hatband. Others are specific to an organization: "For that kind of information ask a guy with a green badge." Or, sitting around a conference table, we decide from the facial expressions that George is the only one who knows what this is all about— and later we'll ask him.

In a social structure, certain individuals are charged with leadership responsibilities. They may make decisions which affect others. Usually, the flow of information to these decision makers is vital to the health of the organization. Special attention is given to getting the leader the data he needs. Channels must be kept open. Information must be accurate. It must be delivered with speed. Finally, it may be important to guard the security of information flowing to and from the chief. Elaborate precautions may be taken to see that vital information doesn't fall into "the wrong hands." Messages may bear special seals, red tags, "Top Secret" stamps. And the red phone will be "the hot line."

Encoding

The decoding skills and activities have their counterpart in encoding. The group member must be able to decode the cues which tell him who's in and who's out. Similarly, he must be able to encode the cues which tell others that he's in, or wants in, or wants out. He must be able to decode the status cues of those above or below in the hierarchy. And he must be able to encode the appropriate cues about his own status. He must indicate when he will lead and when he will defer to the leadership of others. Finally, he must be able to decode—and encode—feelings. He wants to predict the emotional climate ahead. And he needs to be able to give storm warnings when his own feelings are gathering force.

Again, the leader or the individual in a special role may require special encoding skills. The socioemotional leader may need to communicate positive feelings—reassurance, affection, inclusion. In the family, this may be the mother. In the business setting, it may be the boss; but it is often someone other than the "task leader." Meanwhile, the task leader may need to communicate other qualities: confidence, assurance, competence. In some groups he may be able to hold his leadership position only if he can give cues of being competitive, hard-driving, and even ruthless. Frequently, the leader faces a delicate balance in his encoding activities. He must present enough status cues so that there is no question about his authority. Yet, in our culture, he can't seem to enjoy his power too much. An ostentatious display of status can lead to resistance and open rebellion.

Frequently, the group gives special nonverbal recognition to individuals in particular roles. The gatekeeper is likely to wear a uniform. So is the enforcer, or, in fact, anyone who has special sanctions to use force, such as the policeman or the soldier. The executive has a spacious office, often high up in the building, with a good view. The furnishings befit his status. There may be original oil paintings on the wall. And as the advertising slogan says, "A title on the door means a rug on the floor." In many bureaucracies, the distribution of these symbols is carefully spelled out. A certain rank gets a certain size office, a particular kind of desk, a certain number of chairs, a given number of ashtrays.

In summary, when we see man in social settings we begin to see behaviors which are not patterned merely by physiological needs or personality traits. Man manipulates nonverbal signs to provide social messages—about his membership in groups, about his role as leader or follower, about his feelings toward other human beings.

THE CULTURAL SYSTEM

Man the world over has language. Similarly, in all cultures he has art, family institutions, religion. He has patterns of work and play, habits of eating and dressing. But just as languages differ, so do man's other culturally patterned activities.

Out of man's rich store of nonverbal cues some are selected out for symbolic manipulation. In any culture, we find a normal distribution of physiological attributes: intelligence, strength, talent. Similarly, we find a range of personality types. But in every culture, some qualities are fostered and encouraged while others are ignored or disparaged. In a Scandinavian village, everyone learns to ski. In a South Sea Isle, everyone learns to swim. In war-like tribes, aggressive personalities are encouraged and rewarded. In other cultures, the nurturing personality may have the most honored place. The individual learns, within his own culture, the appropriate cues to signal his membership, to indicate his role as man or woman, parent or child, chief or follower. He learns the cues required to validate himself as a "human being."

Decoding

The child's experience in decoding nonverbal cues starts early in life. Cultures differ in child-rearing practices, in the way the infant is socialized. But the earliest social experiences are nonverbal. They involve touch and smell, taste and sight. They include sounds, hums and murmurs, and words which do not yet mean words. In some cultures, infant care is very tactile. The mother's warmth is given freely. The child is fondled. He exists in a rich environment of odors, tastes, sounds, and colors. In other cultures, children are swaddled to inhibit movement. They are fed on prescribed schedules. They are handled only when necessary.

As a child matures, he quickly learns to decode those cues related to his sex role. He learns that men don't cry, but that girls may. Or, in a different culture, he learns that it is the men who do the ceremonial weeping, a privilege not granted to females. He learns that boys don't hold hands, but girls may. Or, if he grows up in many parts of Africa and the Middle East, he learns that male hand-holding is a perfectly acceptable sign of friendship. He learns who to kiss, where, and when. He learns how to walk like a man and dress like a man. To the outsider, his skirt or kilt may look very unmasculine, but in his culture it may be *the* male dress.

Processing

The culturally learned cues have fantastic power. They are overlearned, often without realization that there *could* be any alternative. For that reason, they tend to be far out of awareness. The individual may have great difficulty indicating the cues that he notes, the inferences he makes, the whys of his own behavior. Similarly, when he sees a violation of his expectations he is likely to react with strong emotions. When he sees two males holding hands he is likely to react with disgust and aversion, even if he knows intellectually that in another culture this doesn't signal homosexuality. In many cultures, the name for the tribe is the same as the word for "man" or "human being." The people who do not speak my language are not "really human." And similarly, those who do not have the meanings I do for nonverbal cues must be inhuman, or not normal.

Just as there appear to be differences between "visualizers" and "verbalizers" at the individual level, there may be similar orientations within whole cultures. Researchers, for example, have been intrigued with what is known as "eidetic imagery"—the ability to recall visual scenes with startling "photographic memory." Anecdotal evidence suggests that certain primitive tribes were remarkably high in this ability. And some scholars have speculated that it may be a characteristic skill in preliterate societies but a facility that fades when man can begin to rely on writing.

In a somewhat similar vein of speculation, scholars have contrasted Catholic and Protestant cultures or cultures dominated by Eastern as opposed to Western religions. It has been pointed out, for example, that Protestant cultures were very suspicious of "sensual" delights. The Puritan ethics did not, for example, condone stained glass windows, artistic likenesses, statues, incense, or colorful robes. Similarly, the Judeo-Christian tradition generally has seen a sharp cleavage between mind (which produces rational words) and body (which produces irrational longings and other "sinful" nonverbal messages). Thus, it has been argued, whole cultures may be shaped toward or away from processing certain types of cues.

Encoding

Within a culture, the sanctions for poor encoding are great. When a man is ejected from a group, he may find another group. But when he is tossed out of his culture, it is like being expelled from the human race. It is not a risk one takes lightly.

Problems in encoding often occur between generations, particularly if the parents have emigrated from another culture. Increasingly, we see the problem in any culture in rapid transition. A few years ago the American culture suffered such a shock wave when men began to let their hair grow long, their beards come out, their figures be seen. Men also took to colorful and outlandish clothes, instead of the traditional dull male plumage. Meanwhile, girls began wearing miniskirts and see-through blouses. To many members of the older generation this was all very disturbing. When they learned to encode their nonverbal symbols, you could "tell the boys from the girls." And the girls, when you saw them, were "modest" and "proper" instead of "promiscuous" and "blatant."

SUMMARY

This chapter examined the decoding, processing, and encoding of nonverbal markers at four different levels of prediction: the physiological, the psychological, the social, and the cultural. As a physical creature, man has a certain range of capacities, a set of needs, an ability to reduce uncertainty through sign processes. He also exhibits the capacity to learn. This learning, in turn, shapes the markers he will produce, the cues he will notice, the symbolic assignments he will make. Some sign behaviors are learned by everyone within a culture. Others are learned by people in certain roles or in certain groups. And some behaviors develop out of unique personal experience.

Against this backdrop, we can now examine man's individual code systems.

DISCUSSION–EXERCISES

1. Examine the nonverbal messages you encode in a day. Can you identify some which arise at (a) the cultural level? (b) the social level? (c) the psychological level? (d) the physiological level?

2. Think about your interactions with the very young and the very old. In what ways do they differ from young adults? How does this affect their communication behavior?

3. Think about two friends you know quite well. What can you predict about their communication behavior from knowing their personalities?

4. Try to observe a father and a mother with their child. Does the father act differently than the mother toward the child? How? Does the child act differently with the two parents? How?

5. Find a message printed outside the United States (e.g., a German magazine, a British newspaper, the instructions from a Japanese product). Can you detect any cultural differences in the message? What are they?

PART III

CODES

6

performance 1: human sounds

LEARNING TIPS

In the next three chapters we shall take a closer look at performance codes. This chapter begins with an elaboration of types of performance codes. Then it moves on to deal with signs produced by the human voice. The chapter will

1. Introduce you to the following kinds of performance codes:

   - emblems
   - illustrators
   - regulators
   - affect displays
   - adaptors

2. Alert you to nonverbal cues that are:

   - enduring
   - temporary
   - momentary

3. Introduce you to the following terms from the area of "paralanguage" and "extralinguistics":

   - voice qualities
     - range
     - resonance
     - tempo
     - control
   - vocal segregates
   - vocal qualifiers
     - intensity
     - pitch height
     - extent
   - vocal characterizers

THOUGHT STARTERS

1. How many nonverbal sounds can you produce?

2. Describe the voice of a friend.

3. Say "That's nice" as many different ways as you can.

"Hello, is Xantippe there?"

"This is she." She had a low, seductive voice.

"Oh . . . ah . . . Hi . . . My name is Bill. . . ." His voice cracked in a squeak reminiscent of adolescence.

"Bill . . .?"

"Yes . . . well . . . umm . . . you don't know me . . . but I'm Al's roommate. . . ."

"Al?"

"Yeah . . . umm . . . you met him the other night . . . uhh . . . tall, handsome guy. . . ." He found himself motioning toward his roommate even though his listener could not see his gesture.

"Oh, that Al."

"Yes, well . . . umm . . . he seemed to think you were very nice. . . ." (That was a dumb thing to say, he thought, but he pushed on.) "And . . . umm . . . he thought I might enjoy meeting you, too . . . um . . . and, well, I'm not doing any- ..thing tonight . . . and . . . ah . . . I thought . . . I thought maybe if you weren't doing anything . . . ah . . . hello, are you still there?"

"Yes."

WITH HIS PERFORMANCE CODES, with minimal movements and slight sounds, man can produce a vast array of markers. These markers, in turn, are likely to have strong sign value for another person. They may say much about the person who produces them. They tell what kind of person he is. How rewarding he will be to interact with. How costly. His current state. His past experiences.

As suggested earlier, the efficient communicator is likely to focus on those signs that: (a) reduce large amounts of uncertainty, (b) reduce important kinds of uncertainty, (c) reduce uncertainty which cannot be reduced via other signs, and (d) reduce uncertainty with a minimum of effort for the receiver. On all these scores, the performance codes are a rich source of information.

Looking at another human being, we may conclude that the individual will interact or he won't. We may make inferences about status, who would be dominant and who would be subordinate in potential interaction. We may be able to gauge the cost—and the rewards—of interacting with this type of individual. Once in an interaction, performance cues are likely to provide signs about the individual's inner states. Is he happy? Sincere? Enthusiastic? Skeptical? Angry? All these signs may be available while other events are taking place, while the verbal band is being fully used. And, monitoring performance cues takes minimal effort in interaction. A slight movement of the eyes, and the receiver has garnered a store of markers, to sift and sort, to interpret and apply.

Performance codes are grouped simply by how the markers are produced; they arise from movements or sounds of the human body. Additional groupings can be made on the basis of use—the function played by the signs in human interaction. In terms of the ABX-X' model, nonverbal signs may communicate (a) content, information about the Xs outside the communication system, or (b) relationships, information about the A-to-B dimension, news about the sources, the receivers, and their mutual system.

Working particularly on facial expressions and body movements, Paul Ekman and Wallace Friesen have made more refined groupings on the basis of (a) origin, (b) coding, and (c) use.[1] We will introduce the same scheme here to sharpen our perceptions of performance codes generally. The origin question asks how a particular marker came into man's sign repertoire. How did it come to be produced in the first place? Is it innate? Is it learned within the culture? Within a particular social group or social role? Through idiosyncratic, individual experiences? Then how does it come to have sign value in human communication? Are meanings panhuman, the same for men everywhere? Or are they learned within a culture? Or within a social group? Or via individual, personal experience? Next, the coding question asks to what extent the sign is like its referent. To what extent is it iconic as opposed to arbitrary, analogic as opposed to digital? Finally, the use question asks about the role of the sign in interaction. How does it relate to verbal signs? Is it completely independent? Is it intimately related, so that it reinforces, or supplements, or con-

---

[1] Paul Ekman and Wallace V. Friesen, "The Repertoire of Nonverbal Behavior: Categories, Usage, and Coding," *Semiotica*, 1, 1969, pp. 49–98.

tradicts? And, where does the marker's use fit in the total interaction pattern? Does it play a particular role in the formation stage? In moving the participants toward problem solutions? In maintaining or terminating the interaction?

TYPES OF PERFORMANCE CODES

On the basis of origin, coding, and use, Ekman and Friesen distinguish five classes of performance codes: (a) emblems, (b) illustrators, (c) regulators, (d) affect displays, and (e) adaptors.

Emblems

Emblems are highly stylized nonverbal signs or sign patterns which are widely understood within the user's culture or subculture. Examples include the hitchhiker's thumbing, the A-Okay sign, and the two-finger peace gesture. Emblems can be easily translated into a word or phrase. They can exist alone, without any direct relationship to verbal signs. However, they may also be used to reinforce, supplement, or countermand information in the verbal band. For example, one might reinforce the verbal message "Great!" by making the A-Okay sign. On the other hand, one could countermand the same positive word by adding an obscene gesture, such as "the finger." Emblems appear to be learned very much the way language vocabulary is learned. And they are usually performed with awareness and with an intent to communicate a specifiable message.

Illustrators

Illustrators are nonverbal signs and sign patterns which are used in conjunction with verbal signs. They index and signal. They provide a nonverbal commentary on events in the verbal band. They accentuate, clarify, specify, amplify, punctuate, underscore. Several types of illustrators have been distinguished. Some, for example, point to objects. Others show the shape of objects. Others trace the flow of ideas racing through the mind of the encoder. In all, six major types of illustrators have been identified: (a) pointers, (b) pictographs, (c) ideographs, (d) spatials, (e) kinetographs, and (f) batons. These will be discussed in greater detail in Chapter Eight. Illustrators may be performed with intent. They may be done with the expectation that they will help the receiver understand better. They may also, however, be done with little awareness. The encoder may not realize the extent to which he is "talking with his hands."

Regulators

Regulators are nonverbal signs and sign patterns that regulate inter-action in a communication system. Examples include head nods, eye contact, gestures indicating one wishes to speak, or gestures requesting the other person to respond. They comment on the relationship. They provide feedback that tells each participant how the interaction is going, what needs to be done next, when changes need to occur. They provide a flow of traffic signals to ensure a smooth-running communication system. Regulators are performed efficiently by all members within a culture. But usually the participants have little awareness of the regulators being produced or the effects they are having.

Affect Displays

Affect displays are nonverbal signs or sign patterns which indicate emotional states. They may be involuntary (i.e., symptoms of an internal state). Or, they may be performed on purpose, as symbols in interaction. The face is the prime region of affect display, although total body configuration may be a cue to positive and negative emotions. Ekman and Friesen have produced evidence that affect displays are panhuman. Men around the world will produce similar facial markers when feeling a particular emotion. At the same time, cultures differ in their "display rules," what is appropriate and inappropriate to exhibit; in growing up, children learn what emotions to mask, deintensify, intensify, or neutralize. In addition, a communicator may simulate an affect display, putting on a happy face when he is not pleased, showing a grief-saddened face when he really is pleased. This may be done in an attempt to fool someone—or with the open acknowledgement that it is an act, a symbolic performance.

Adaptors

Adaptors are nonverbal markers that originated in the satisfaction of self needs, such as eating, cleansing oneself, scratching an itch, or rubbing tired eyes. Over time, however, they have become part of the individual's habit repertoire. They may be produced in adult life, in abbreviated form, quite divorced from their original need-fulfilling context. They may suddenly emerge when an individual is feeling tense, or tired, or particularly relaxed and satisfied. The producer usually does not create the adaptor with the intent of communicating. The production may, in fact, be done with little awareness. But, for the observer, the adaptor may have sign value; it may be an informative indicator of the performer's inner state.

ENDURING, TEMPORARY, AND
MOMENTARY MARKERS

In studying nonverbal cues we encounter a factor we do not usually consider in verbal language. A primary feature of speech is the "fast-fading" nature of each sign. The sound is emitted and then disappears. This, in turn, clears the verbal band for succeeding signs. It makes speech a rapid and efficient system which can encode a vast range of very different messages in a very brief period.

In contrast, some nonverbal signs endure for long periods. A monument, for example, may be a nonverbal symbol that stands there sending the same message century after century. It is made the way it is so it will *not* be a rapid-fading sign. Some nonverbal cues are, of course, as momentary as a spoken word. Facial expressions may change in less time than it takes to speak a word.

In general, it will be helpful to note that nonverbal signs may be (a) *enduring*, (b) *temporary*, or (c) *momentary*. The enduring markers are those that, like monuments or architecture, may continue for long periods, beyond the life of one communication system, perhaps beyond the life of the participants. Or, at a more individual level, the enduring markers may include the general appearance of the person: how big he is, how his face and body are structured, what he looks like day in and day out. These markers move with the individual from communication system to communication system. They may have an impact on interaction, but they are not specific to any one situation.

The temporary markers are those that do change over time, but that may be stable during one communication situation, or during a phase of interaction. The seating arrangement at a meeting, for example, could be set up in a number of different ways. But once organized, it is likely to remain the same during the whole meeting, or at least during much of the meeting. Similarly, the clothing people wear may change from day to day, but is likely to remain the same during one interaction. Finally, individuals may have moods or other states that change from one day to another but don't change moment to moment. On a particular day, I may be feeling very good—or bad—and that happiness or sadness may influence all of my interactions.

The momentary markers are those that, like the spoken word, change from instant to instant. Facial expressions and hand movements are prime examples. They may shift many times during a single interaction.

In all these areas, signs can be produced that are signals or symbols, cues to other succeeding events, or markers that indicate other referents.

Often the enduring and temporary markers are unpremeditated; we don't plan them on purpose. Yet many, such as seating arrangement, can be organized to prestructure the communication system, the interaction which is likely to occur.

In summary, so far in this chapter we have begun to examine performance codes more closely. We have suggested that the myriad markers produced by the human body may be categorized—according to origin, according to coding, according to use. In particular, we have introduced emblems, illustrators, regulators, affect displays, and adaptors. In addition, we have noted that markers, in the performance codes and perhaps in other codes, may be enduring, temporary, or momentary. Now we begin to examine areas of performance code, starting with the human voice, then moving on to the face, the hands, the total body. In the rest of the chapter we shall focus on human sounds. It is here that the verbal and nonverbal most intimately interweave. It is here that we can see most clearly the power of each.

HUMAN SOUNDS

The human animal makes many sounds simply in being alive. Some signal his inner states; they are symptoms of contentment or distress, health or sickness. His heart beats. And it quickens its pace when he is excited. The steady sound of his breathing may shift to the gasp of surprise, the sigh of resignation, the yawn of boredom, or the snore of slumber. His tummy rumbles when he is hungry. And when he has eaten, his digestive system may make other noises; he may hiccup, burp, belch, and expel gas. He may sniffle, sneeze, and cough when he is getting a cold. And he may pant when he is too hot. Even his movements produce sounds: the staccato click of a brisk walk, the shuffle of fatigue, the stomp of anger, or the drumming of impatient fingers.

When he is happy, he may hum or whistle, just as a contented kitten purrs. When a performance pleases him, he may clap his hands. When he is displeased, he may click his tongue. When he wants to attract attention, he may snap his fingers. All these are sounds unassisted by implement. If he has a drum or a flute or a gavel he can produce an even wider range of noise. And all these sounds are in addition to the human noise that usually concerns us most: speech, the product of human voice.

When we move to speech we are at the heart of verbal communication. Historically, for civilization and for the individual, speech precedes writing. But when we learn to read and write we often begin to think of verbal communication as we see it on the printed page, neatly segmented into sentences, with capital letters at the beginning and periods at the end. Actually, written language only hints at some of the important features of speech. It suggests, but does not capture, intonations, stress, and pauses. This is readily apparent when we read a written passage aloud. There's a striking difference between the actor who reads "with expression" and the reader who delivers a string of words in dull monotone. The latter captures what is on the printed page, but he doesn't "add" what we usually get in speech.

Classically, the linguistic scholar was concerned with recording and analyzing the verbal code. He wanted to be able to describe it. He wanted to be able to compare languages. He wanted to trace their evolution over time. The focus was on the central system, divorced from the individual speaker, shed of idiosyncrasies, extracted from the social context.

Paralanguage

Recently, however, linguists have begun to concern themselves with *paralanguage*, or the language alongside of language. Another term for this area is "extralinguistic." It includes features such as voice quality, pitch, range, and other sounds that may punctuate the verbal stream (e.g., grunts and groans). With the printed word, scholars have similarly become concerned with *typography*, the style of lettering, the size of type, the layout and display of different print configurations.

In our definition of nonverbal communication, the areas of paralanguage and typography fall on the borderline between the verbal and the nonverbal domains. They are intimately related to linguistic signs. But they are auxiliary to the signs and sign patterns that usually occupy the language scholar.

Most people have trouble coming to grips with "paralanguage" the first time they bump into the concept. It *is* slippery if you have not had a little background in linguistic analysis. So let's try this example. Let's say you had someone record a simple phrase or sentence, such as: "That is very nice." If you then let people listen to this record, they would probably agree that this is an English sentence, that it has a particular meaning, that the speaker intended to communicate a certain message. *In addition*, however, the listeners would be able to tell you other things about your speaker. They could probably tell whether the speaker was male or female. They could detect whether he was British or American. They might be able to tell you whether he was young or old, nervous or calm. And, they might say other things about him. He's sexy. Or, he's tired. He's happy. Or, he's angry. Whatever it is that allows people to make such inferences: *that's* paralanguage. In the next section we'll examine more carefully just what it is that allows us to make such inferences.

VOCAL CUES

The production of vocal sounds requires a careful orchestration of lips, tongue, teeth, larynx, respiration. Upon inspection it turns out to be a surprisingly complex phenomenon. We do it all the time. And we do it without thought. But to most of us, a speech sound just comes out "right"—or it doesn't. We'd be hard put to diagnose just why one vocal sound was different from another, or why one "sounds funny."

Similarly, in describing the voice of a friend, we're probably aware that the voice is high or low (e.g., a soprano vs. a bass). We may note that some people are consistently loud whereas others are soft-spoken. And there may be other dimensions which are somewhat harder to describe; for example, one person may have a resonant voice while another person's is less "full-bodied."

Voice Qualities

In paralanguage a half-dozen "voice qualities" are used to distinguish voice patterns. These are illustrated in Figure 6-1. First is *range*. Some individuals use a wide range of pitch; others speak in a narrow band, in extreme cases approaching a monotone. As part of our normal linguistic production, we raise our voice when asking a question and we drop our voice at the end of a statement. But for some individuals this drop or rise is small; for others it represents a major change of pitch.

Second is *resonance*. In large part this arises from the individual's vocal equipment. It always seems amusing, in a cartoon or comedy, to see a very tiny boy with a great big booming voice. Similarly, a thin, wispy voice is surprising in a hulking adult male. The third voice quality is *tempo*, the speed of vocal production. This may be either increased or decreased from "normal" speed. In short, some individuals speak very rapidly, others very slowly. And, of course, the same individual may increase his tempo when he is excited or aroused.

Fourth is *control*. Actually, three different types of control can be distinguished. First is lip control, the manipulations which produce smooth transitions as opposed to sharp transitions. Second is articulation control, which leads to a forced as opposed to a relaxed stream of sound. Third is rhythm control, which produces a smooth flowing rhythm as opposed to a jerky, broken rhythm.

Voice qualities, particularly as we have discussed them here, refer to enduring markers, cues which may distinguish one speaker from another. It is from cues such as these that we make inferences about an individual's age and background, his status and social class, his vitality and re-

FIGURE 6-1   Voice Qualities.

In paralanguage, several types of voice quality are distinguished: (A) pitch range, (B) resonance, (C) tempo, and (D) control, which includes lip control, articulation control, and rhythm control.

Figure 6-2 Vocal Qualifiers.

A. INTENSITY

B. PITCH HEIGHT

C. EXTENT

Vocal qualifiers include (A) intensity, such as overloud or oversoft; (B) pitch height, such as overhigh or overlow; (C) extent, such as clipping or drawing.

sponsiveness. We have all seen instances, of course, where someone makes a temporary change in speech production. A shift occurs in a particular communication situation, for example in making a speech in front of the class, in interviewing for a job, or in meeting an important individual. Someone who is normally animated and vivacious may suddenly freeze into a restricted monotone. The voice may fade away until it is almost too soft to hear, or the speaker may "swallow" words or the ends of sentences.

Vocal Qualifiers

In paralanguage, three vocal qualifiers are distinguished. Frequently these are temporary changes. They shift with the topic under discussion or with the communication situation. First is *intensity*: the vocal production may be overloud or oversoft. Second is *pitch height*: the vocal stream may be overhigh or overlow. Third is what is called *extent*: this includes phenomena such as drawling and clipping. Figure 6-2 illustrates these patterns.

Characterizers and Segregates

In traditional paralinguistics two final categories round out the description of speech production. *Vocal characterizers* give temporary or momentary cues about the communicator and his interaction. Whispering, for example, is a "vocal characterizer." This in turn may suggest that the communicator is transmitting confidential information. Or he is drawing the boundary of his communication system in a tight circle, excluding those farther out in his environment. Similarly, yelling is a vocal characterizer that extends the boundary of the communication system. Laughing, moaning, and whining are other vocal characterizers which give clues to the quality and content of the interaction.

Finally, *vocal segregates* are momentary interjections into the stream of speech. Examples include pauses and such sounds as uh, umm, and ah. They are closely related to the somewhat broader category of *speech nonfluencies*. (The latter includes starting the same sentence twice, as Bill did: "I thought . . . I thought maybe. . . ." Or it includes broken thoughts, where the speaker starts one sentence and then jumps to another without completing the first: for example, "Al said you were very . . . I wanted to call because. . . .")

Vocal segregates and nonfluencies have been studied extensively in speech communication. As you would expect, such disruptions tend to increase when a speaker is under stress. They, in turn, are likely to be interpreted by a listener as symptoms of stress, and this may reduce the speaker's credibility. The speaker may seem less competent and less effective than he would otherwise. Most damaging, of course, is the instance where the stress is seen as arising from deception. The listener may decide the speaker is "hemming and hawing" because he doesn't want to reveal the truth or because he is having difficulty fabricating a smooth presentation of a nontruth.

FUNCTIONS OF SOUND

The vocal cues identified in paralanguage and extralinguistics serve useful functions in human communication. They help regulate interaction; they comment on the state of the communicators and their communication system. The category system introduced at the beginning of this chapter was generated primarily to deal with facial expressions and hand gestures. But the same classification scheme helps point up the way vocal cues are used.

Vocal Affect Displays

As we will see in Chapter 7, the face is perhaps the most effective displayer of emotion. But vocal cues—above and beyond the words selected—can be significant indicators of emotion. In fact, Albert Mehrabian has performed experiments in which he introduced conflicts among the verbal content, the accompanying vocal cues, and facial expressions.[2] From these experiments, he concludes that, in the communication of feelings, the words themselves only account for about 7 percent of the impact. Meanwhile, the vocal cues produce 38 percent of the effect, and facial expressions contribute a whopping 55 percent. In short, you can say you like something or that you don't like it, that you're happy or that you're not happy, but unless your voice and face match your words —don't be surprised if people don't believe you.

Many ingenious studies have been done on the recognition of emotion from vocal cues.[3] With modern technology it is possible to scramble speech so that the content is completely disguised—but the paralanguage qualities remain. These electronically processed tapes in turn can be played in different cultures to see if the same personality and emotion judgments are made from language to language.

It is not surprising, of course, to be able to detect emotion from voices even when you can't make out the words. Perhaps you have had a

---

[2] Albert Mehrabian, *Silent Messages* (Belmont, Calif.: Wadsworth, 1971), pp. 42–47.

[3] Klaus Scherer, J. Koivumaki, and R. Rosenthal, "Minimal Cues in the Vocal Communication of Affect," *Journal of Psycholinguistic Research*, 1 (3), 1972, pp. 269–285.

real life experience with "filtered speech"—for example, hearing voices from next door in a motel, hotel, or apartment. Usually it's impossible to hear individual words. But from paralinguistic cues you may be able to tell whether the participants are having a fight—or a party.

Usually, in our culture, as anger builds up, voices become louder and louder. Just before blows are struck, the participants are likely to be yelling at each other at the top of their voices. In some cultures, however, an opposite pattern exists. As anger builds up, voices become softer and softer. The greatest danger is when things get *very* quiet. This has surprised more than a few Americans who find themselves in the middle of a slugfest which occurred "completely out of the blue."

Vocal Emblems

The most obvious vocal counterpart of an "emblem" is: the word. There are a few examples, however, of vocal sounds that are not words (or at least do not appear in the dictionary) but approach emblem status. Included would be sounds of disapproval such as the "tsk, tsk" clicking of the tongue or the "harumph" grunt. In more bucolic and chauvinistic days, young men (then called "wolves") would stand around on street corners whistling at girls with a characteristic sound of appraisal and appreciation. Another vocal emblem might be Charlie Brown's cry of frustration: "Augh!"

Vocal Illustrators

We can similarly find examples of vocal "illustration" although many vocal cues of this nature are intimate parts of the linguistic pattern. If, for example, inflection goes up at the end of a phrase, the meaning is changed from a statement to a question. The stressing of one word over another introduces subtle shifts in meaning. For example, "*I* should go." (I, rather than someone else, should go.) "I *should* go." (I should, but I don't want to.) "I should *go*." (Go rather than do something else.) Perhaps the simplest examples of vocal illustrators are where we use the voice to imitate a sound. "The engine went: 'brrr . . ca-chunk . . ca-chunk!'" Or, "The lion went: 'rraaRRrrr!'" Or, "Suddenly, the whole thing went 'Kaa-BOOM!'"

Vocal Regulators

Many vocal cues influence interaction. They trigger responses. They affect the duration of utterances. They control latency of response, how long it takes for one speaker to pick up after another has finished. They pace and regulate the rate of interaction. Typically, a change of inflection signals the end of an utterance and an opportunity for the listener to speak. If inflection goes up, as at the end of a question, the listener is expected to respond. Similarly, a drop of inflection at the end of a statement, followed by a pause, usually triggers a comment from the listener. Usually, he must speak, acknowledging that he has been listening or perhaps is still decoding. The listener may respond simply with a head nod. Or, he may let his eyes roll up as if thinking. Here the vocal cues are intimately intertwined with the nonverbal signals. If, for example, the speaker combines a change in inflection with a pause—but also includes an upward eye movement—then the listener is *not* expected to respond. The speaker has indicated that he is thinking or searching and he will continue in a moment. Similarly, some of the vocal segregates—such as umm, ah, uh—serve to "hold the floor" for a speaker. They give him a chance to reflect, to process feedback, to collect his thoughts. But they signal his desire to continue in just a moment. As with gestural regulators, these patterns of vocal regulation are well known to everyone in a culture, yet we don't "know we know." They tend to be far out of awareness.

Vocal Adaptors

Many of man's sounds serve very useful biological functions. We laugh, or cry, or snort, or cough, or sigh, or swallow. These activities help us readjust our biological equipment. Sometimes, however, these same sounds are produced on purpose, as symbols. We laugh derisively, or we snort, to communicate our scorn. We may cough to signal to someone that he is dealing with a sensitive topic, perhaps to warn him that he is about to reveal a secret. Or, we may clear our throat as a signal. Al did this in his first exchange with Bill. He wanted to attract Bill's attention, and indeed Bill looked up. Clearing the throat is a common preparation for speaking. It is done unconsciously, for the very practical reason that it will make later verbal encoding easier. We have all learned that it is an adaptor which signals the approach of speech. But it can also be used as a purposeful symbol. If we enter a room and someone is not aware of us, we may clear the throat, not because we wish to speak, but simply because we want to call attention to our presence.

SUMMARY

This chapter begins our exploration of the performance codes. We noted that, on the basis of origin, coding, and use, we can make a further breakdown in our classification of nonverbal signs. We distinguished among (a) emblems, word-like nonverbal symbols; (b) illustrators, nonverbal signs which elaborate on verbal symbols; (c) regulators, nonverbal signs which signal changes in the communication system; (d) affect displays, signs which indicate emotion; and (e) adaptors, once-useful movements which now may reveal inner states. We also noted that nonverbal cues may be (a) enduring, continuing for long periods of time; (b) temporary, changing but perhaps constant during one interaction; and (c) momentary, shifting rapidly from instant to instant.

Against this background, we began examining human sounds, particularly touching on those vocal cues studied in "paralanguage" or "extralinguistics." We noted that voice qualities differ, along such dimensions as range, resonance, tempo, and control. In a given communication situation, vocal qualifiers may be heard, in shifts in intensity, pitch height, and extent. Vocal characterizers may color the message further, with whispering, yelling, groaning, and so on. Finally, vocal segregates and other nonfluencies may introduce pauses and nonlinguistic sounds (such as "ah" and "umm") into the verbal stream. We concluded with examples of vocal cues in use, applying our classification system: emblems, illustrators, regulators, affect displays, and adaptors. We are now ready to leave the vocal and the verbal and apply this category scheme to the face, hands, and body.

DISCUSSION–EXERCISES

1. Can you think of additional examples of vocal emblems? Vocal regulators? Vocal adaptors?

2. Say aloud: "That is very nice." Now repeat it, each time placing the emphasis on a different word. Does the meaning change as you shift emphasis?

3. Repeat "That is very nice," trying to express these emotions: happiness, surprise, sadness, anger, fear, disgust. How successful were you? What changed as you moved from emotion to emotion?

4. Repeat "That is very nice," using different accents: British, French, German, Italian, Swedish, Russian, Oriental. How successful were you? What changed as you moved from accent to accent?

5. Repeat "That is very nice," imitating an old man, a shy young woman, a boisterous drunk. What changed as you moved from imitation to imitation?

performance 2:
the human face

LEARNING TIPS

This chapter is designed to

1. Introduce you to four types of cues in the area of the head and face:
   - appearance cues
   - eye behavior
   - facial expressions
   - head movements

2. Alert you to cues which are (a) enduring, (b) semifixed, and (c) momentary—and to their value in communication systems.

3. Introduce you to the primary affect displays, the expressions of emotion which appear universally: happiness, sadness, surprise, anger, fear, and disgust.

4. Orient you to problems in emotion recognition, and in sorting simulated from felt affects: the problems of partials, blends, micros, and timing.

5. Draw your attention to eye behavior: pupil dilation, direction of gaze, and mutual glances in interaction.

THOUGHT STARTERS

1. How well can you read the facial expressions of others?

2. How well can you regulate communication with your own facial cues?

3. Take the test in Figure 7-1.

4. Have a friend give you the test in Appendix B-2.

She had a pretty face.
He raised his eyebrows and smiled.
"I'm Bill."
She nodded. "Hi. I'm Xan."

The head and face are perhaps man's richest sign system. In Western culture, the head is frequently used in art to represent the whole man; it is seen as the locus of his personality, his intelligence, his soul. The face is central in most communication situations. In fact, we speak of "face-to-face" communication. Or, the face is used symbolically, as in "face the music," or tragically, "losing face." The head is the locus of most of the primary sense receptors: eyes, ears, nose, mouth—seeing, hearing, smelling, tasting. By looking at a person's head we know whether he is awake or asleep, listening, smelling, tasting, hearing. Vocalizations come out of the mouth. Facial expressions play across the features. And we tend to read a man's physiognomy for his history—his genetic heritage, his time on this earth, and the way that time has marked his character. This chapter examines areas of performance code in the head and face: (a) appearance cues, (b) facial expressions, (c) eye behavior, and (d) head nods and movements.

APPEARANCE CUES

As with the voice, the head and face present some cues which are enduring, some which are semifixed or situation-specific, and some which are momentary or fleeting. The enduring cues reveal demographic data: the individual's age, sex, race, possibly ethnic and national origins, possibly status or occupation. The cues include: baldness, gray hair, wrinkles, muscle tone and fat deposits, pigmentation of the skin, color of the eyes, the shape and configuration of features. The semifixed markers are less permanent. But they are likely to remain constant during one interaction. Cues include the length of hair and the way it is styled, the degree to which the individual is shaved or not shaved, the way eyebrows are plucked, how clean the individual is. The semifixed markers are likely to signal the individual's concepts about beauty, his reference groups, his self-perceived or desired status. They may indicate his definition of a communication situation: for formal groups he is combed and shaved and scrubbed; for informal gatherings he is less meticulous. Finally, the momentary markers are the fleeting facial expressions: the raised eyebrow, the curled lip, the snort, the lowered eyes. They signal emotions. They are likely to be read for interest or boredom, for belief or skepticism, for signs of acceptance or rejection.

Enduring Markers

Because they are difficult to change, the enduring markers make relatively inefficient codes for the producer, but effective codes for the observer. The producer has three options: (1) he can choose to reveal the marker; (2) he can conceal the marker; or (3) he can mask the marker, changing it into a different cue. Some people are proud of their gray hair, their dark skin, their crow's feet, their kinky hair, their unique features. They display these cues and capitalize on them. Jimmy Durante, for example, made a fortune being shot in profile so that you couldn't miss his prominent proboscis.

Some of the enduring markers may be concealed, perhaps with an article of costume, an artifact. The middle-aged lady may wear a scarf, or a high-necked dress, to conceal the unflattering neck wrinkles. Or, like Bing Crosby and Frank Sinatra in their later years, the aging gentleman may take to wearing a hat to conceal the balding pate. Similarly, the aging star may take to wearing dark glasses to help conceal the telltale bags under the eyes.

The masking or changing of an enduring cue is more radical. It may involve an artifact. The girl with stringy hair puts on a wig of flowing locks. The balding man covers up with a toupée. The young lady changes the color of her eyes with contact lenses. But it may require major effort, and even pain: plastic surgery, capping the teeth or replacing them with dentures, dying the hair, face lifts, hair transplants, tanning or bleaching the skin, straightening the hair.

Because the enduring markers are so hard to change, they may be important signs for the observer. They are likely to absorb great uncertainty: about the other person's age, sex, and background. They tend to be reliable.

They may quickly provide information that would be hard to ask for. In the formation stage of interaction, they may play an important role in decisions. Most people find it easiest to interact with people like themselves. It takes less effort. There are fewer unpleasant surprises. It is usually more rewarding. If given a choice, they will often choose to interact with others who are like themselves, in age, in sex, in social status. On the other hand, man sometimes seeks variety. He is attracted to people of beauty, of status, of unique and interesting background. Again, the appearance markers may provide good predictors about the potential rewards and costs of interaction.

Face Reading

The "reading of the face" is an ancient and venerable art, comparable to reading tea leaves, or the palm, or bumps on the head. A legend in the Talmud tells of "the science of physiognomy" in the time of Moses. According to the story, a famous king sent his court painter to capture the likeness of Moses so that his wise men could analyze this famous face and explain to the king what made Moses so great. The king could then cultivate these same qualities in himself. But when the painter returned with the likeness, and the physiognomers studied it, they told the king: "There must be some mistake in this likeness, for we have analyzed it and it represents the worst possible set of characteristics that could be collected in one man's face; each feature reveals some conflicting and terrible flaw of character."

Enraged, the king sent a messenger back to Moses to compare the likeness, thinking, of course, that the painter had badly botched the job. But when Moses heard of the incident, he responded, "Ah no, that is precisely the source of my greatness; I had all the worst possible passions a man could know—and it is out of mastering these conflicting forces that I emerged such a wise and great man."

This story, interestingly enough, has also been told about Socrates and Alexander the Great and perhaps many other great ancients.

In the early days of psychology, a good deal of effort was spent on sweeping away some of the "old wives' tales" that populated folklore. And, of course, notions about being able to read man's character or fate from his facial features was an early target of investigation. For the most part, research did not reveal any systematic relationship between a man's physiognomy and his character, talent, intelligence, or fate. A man with a low forehead was not necessarily low in intelligence. Close-set eyes did not reveal a "criminal type"; and so on. What was surprising about many of these studies, however, was that judges frequently agreed about these cues and their meaning. In other words, you might have a man with a low forehead who was demonstrably a very intelligent individual. But show his picture to a group of judges and they would tend to agree that, yes, this person was not very bright.

This then became a very interesting problem for social psychologists. Why do people have these stereotypes? Are there culturally induced notions about beauty, or ideal types? And what effect do these stereotypes have on individuals? If, for instance, people always look at you and expect that you will be stupid, you may have to be very bright indeed to escape these expectations. Or vice versa. For example, Robert Rosenthal at Harvard recently did a study in which he told teachers that certain students —randomly selected—were going to be "late bloomers" and evince a sudden spurt in IQ during the following year. Rather startlingly, many of these children—given their teacher's expectations—did evidence significant increases in objectively measured IQ during the school year.[1] I have a very bright Ph. D. friend who has a low forehead and a face that would look well on a boxer. I've always thought his appearance was quite an advantage; people are constantly underestimating him—and then he pounces on them when they least expect it.

While the research literature has continued to fail to find any relationship between facial types and character, fate, and the like, the idea is very persistent. And, in some cases, very elaborate theories have been advanced as to why there should be a relationship. The Hungarian psychologist Lipot Szondi, for example, developed a theory of "genotropism" that argued that men are driven to their fates by latent hereditary factors. Further, he argued that these recessive genes would show up in facial features and that you could look at a young man or woman and predict quite well what would happen to this individual later in life. Finally, he contended that people would be attracted to others who had similar latent qualities. Thus, you could, as he did, take photographs of individuals who were known to suffer from various mental disorders or sexual perversions. When shown to someone else, to a judge, the choices made would reveal the judge's own deepseated proclivities. The projective test that Szondi developed is still being used today, although usually now divorced from his original theory.

Recently, a California lawyer has revived many of the ancient physiognomy predictions in a system called "personology." From years of watching people in the courtroom, the attorney argues that he can make good predictions about an individual just from physiognomic cues alone. While this topic continues to arouse speculation and is an amusing party game activity, the research continues to suggest that the inferences people

---

[1] Robert Rosenthal and L. Jackson, *Pygmalion in the Classroom* (New York: Holt, Rinehart and Winston, 1968).

make can be very misleading. From basic features of the face we may be able to tell something of the individual's genetic heritage. We may be able to read from broken noses and cauliflowered ears some of the experiences that have marked his life. And we may be able to make some judgments about his current vitality, his capacity for interaction. But beyond that, the inference process becomes very complex, blending with many cultural stereotypes which may do considerable injustice to the individual human being.

FACIAL EXPRESSIONS

Just as there has been long controversy over what facial features reveal, so there has been a continuing controversy over what facial expressions reveal. More precisely, researchers have asked: (a) Are certain facial movements related to specific emotions; (b) and, if so, can the average person accurately judge what those facial affects are? Over the past one hundred years, most of the research has focused on the expression of emotion. But recently, investigators have also begun to look at other functions of facial expression. Does, for instance, facial expression serve to regulate interaction? Can facial expressions punctuate conversations or express other meanings?

Affect Displays

An early pioneer was Charles Darwin. After his historic treatise on the evolution of the species, Darwin wrote a book entitled *The Expression of the Emotions in Man and Animals*.[2] A surprisingly good, scientific endeavor, the book represents Darwin's attempt to systematically explore facial expressions. He asked how they differed—and were similar—among men and animals, and among different peoples, around the world. In general, Darwin argued that human facial expressions have their roots in animal behavior; many of the expressions seen in man arose for very practical purposes in lower animals. He thus expected that facial expressions of emotion would be the same around the world. While some of Darwin's notions have not stood the test of time, a surprising number of his predictions have worked out and many are still being explored today, a century after Darwin wrote his original book.[3]

European psychologists tended to follow Darwin's lead, but most

[2] Charles Darwin, *The Expression of the Emotions in Man and Animals* (Chicago: The University of Chicago Press, 1965).
[3] Paul Ekman, *Darwin and Facial Expression: A Century of Research in Review* (New York: Academic Press, 1973).

American psychologists—until very recently—tended to disagree with the father of evolution. The early American findings seemed to indicate that there were few reliable cues in facial affect displays. Further, judges of facial expression seemed to be very poor at discerning what the expressor was really feeling. Among the researchers who did find some regularity, a division grew up between those who thought there were several categories of facially expressed emotion and those who thought that there were a few major dimensions. One early study, for example, found that judges were fairly reliable if you used a few major categories along a continuum: happiness, surprise, fear, anger, suffering, and disgust.[4] Other researchers, however, argued that these expressions could be arranged in a three-dimensional space, with dimensions such as: "pleasant-to-unpleasant" (i.e., happy, smiling faces to sad, crying faces); "attention-to-rejection" (i.e., faces with eyes, mouth, and nostrils open and receptive to stimuli as opposed to faces in which eyes, mouth, and nose appeared to be closed tight as if warding off unpleasant stimuli); and "tension-to-sleep" (i.e., faces that appeared alert, excited, and agitated as opposed to those that appeared relaxed and sleepy).

While the battle still continues between the category approach and the dimensional approach, much of the recent research on facial affect display has been stimulated by a theory of emotion developed by Silvan Tomkins.[5] He argues that the face is a key site of emotion. When an emotion is aroused in an individual, one of the first things that happens is that a neural program fires messages to the face, which, in turn, cause the contraction and relaxation of certain facial muscles. According to Tomkins's theory, the feedback you get from feeling your muscles contract is one of the cues that tells you what emotion you are feeling. Finally, this theory argues that there are unique facial configurations associated with each of the primary affects. The basic emotions identified by Tomkins are (a) interest–excitement, (b) enjoyment–joy, (c) surprise–startle, (d) distress–anguish, (e) shame–humiliation, (f) contempt–disgust, (g) anger–rage, and (h) fear–terror. In each pair, the first is less intense. For each of these affects, with the exception of happiness, there should be one or more unique configurations in each area of the face: brows, eyes, and mouth. Happiness displays itself primarily in the eyes and lower face.

In Tomkins's scheme, the positive emotions center around enjoyment–joy and interest–excitement. Surprise and startle are what Tomkins

⁴ Paul Ekman, Wallace V. Friesen, and Phoebe Ellsworth, *Emotion in the Human Face: Guidelines for Research and an Integration of Findings* (New York: Pergamon Press, 1972). See also C. E. Izard, *The Face of Emotion* (New York: Appleton-Century-Crofts, 1971).

⁵ Silvan S. Tomkins, *Affect, Imagery, Consciousness* (New York: Springer, Vol. I, 1962, Vol. 2, 1963).

calls "re-setting" affects and are not in themselves either positive or negative. Finally, the other affects, such as anguish, disgust, fear, and anger, can be classified as negative emotions. Empirical research has been particularly successful in discriminating cues for surprise, happiness, sadness, disgust, fear, and anger. Increasingly, these basic expressions of emotion have been found around the world, just as Darwin predicted.[6] Figure 7-1 shows a selection of the key cues, in a simplified and somewhat exaggerated form.

FIGURE 7-1   Cues of the Primary Affects.

A. anger   B. sad   C. happy

D. surprise   E. anger   F. sad

G. disgust   H. fear   I. surprise

Can you match the above sketches with the correct affects? (1) happy, (2) sad, (3) surprise, (4) fear, (5) anger, (6) disgust.

Answers: A-5, B-2, C-1, D-3, E-5, F-2, G-6, H-4, I-3.

[6] Paul Ekman, "Universals and Cultural Differences in Facial Expressions of Emotion," in J. Cole (ed.), *Nebraska Symposium on Motivation, 1971* (Lincoln, Nebr.: University of Nebraska Press, 1972), pp. 207–283.

Partials, Blends, and Micros

The full display of an emotion results in muscle movements in all three areas of the face (with the noted exception of happiness, which is reflected primarily in the eyes and mouth). Man can also display *partials*, however. These are expressions in which only one portion of the face is activated. Surprise might, for example, be shown only in a raised brow, or only in a widening of the eyes. In addition, some expressions are *blends*, where one affect, such as happiness, is showing in the mouth, and another affect, such as surprise, is showing in the brow or eye. Finally, some affect displays flit across the features at very fast speeds, for as little as a fifth of a second. These are called micromomentary facial expressions, or *micro-facials*. They are almost impossible for the untrained observer to see with the naked eye. They are, however, very evident in slow motion pictures of the face in action. They show up even when the performer is trying to conceal his feelings—and thinks he has been totally successful. The occurrence of partials, blends, and micros explains, in part, why researchers have had such difficulty in studying the face. It also helps account for the enormous individual differences among people in their ability to recognize and identify facial affect displays.

Display Rules

While recent research indicates that men in all cultures have similar affect displays, people do differ in what they will show in different communication contexts. Figure 7-2 shows a model of affect display that points to the panhuman and the cultural ingredients of facial expressions.

The various affects may be elicited by a variety of stimuli. And depending on learning, different events may trigger joy, fear, surprise, etc. In our culture, for example, the sight of an insect or reptile might stimulate disgust or fear. In another culture, however, the same creature might be an edible delicacy. It might elicit pure joy. If the stimulus is eliciting the same emotion, then the neural program should be the same. This neural message to the face is filtered, however, through one's culturally learned *display rules*. As we grow up, we learn what is appropriate to feel and hence to show. Within a culture, it may be appropriate to *intensify* certain emotional displays. We may not feel much joy at receiving a particular present, but we may intensify what pleasure we do feel, because it is the socially appropriate response. The gift giver expects us to be pleased —and we try to show that we are. On the other hand, there may be occasions when we *deintensify*. It may, for example, be impolite to show how much glee we feel at beating a competitor. We deintensify our display

FIGURE 7-2   Affects and Their Display.

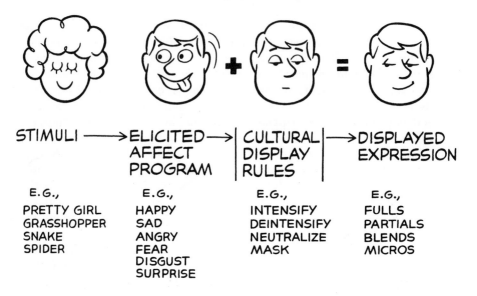

STIMULI ⟶	ELICITED⟶ AFFECT PROGRAM	CULTURAL ⟶ DISPLAY RULES	DISPLAYED EXPRESSION
E.G.,	E.G.,	E.G.,	E.G.,
PRETTY GIRL	HAPPY	INTENSIFY	FULLS
GRASSHOPPER	SAD	DEINTENSIFY	PARTIALS
SNAKE	ANGRY	NEUTRALIZE	BLENDS
SPIDER	FEAR	MASK	MICROS
	DISGUST		
	SURPRISE		

Different stimuli in different cultures may elicit different affects, as a result of learning. But the affect program, once elicited, should be panhuman. Cultures also differ, however, in the "display rules" they impose on expressions.

and only evince mild pleasure. In the middle range, we may *neutralize* expressions, bringing whatever we feel back to an unexpressive "poker face." Finally, some affect displays may require *masking*. The young warrior may be feeling fear but he learns to mask this unwelcome emotion with another, such as anger.

Affect Recognition

The affect displays tend to be important social signals. They help reduce our uncertainties about an important dimension of interaction. We receive early warning when anger is building. We get reassuring messages when our partner is happy. It helps us make important predictions about what will happen next. Similarly, it provides information which is not always easy to get in other ways. We may pick up affect cues from tone of voice, or body posture. But the movements of the face are easily accessible and uniquely reliable. At the same time, it takes skill to interpret facial expressions. It requires seeing the affect display in the first place. Then it requires a complex inference process. It is necessary to decide when the affect is felt, and when it is being simulated without feeling. It is necessary to pick up "false notes" that might indicate masking, or neutralizing, or shifts in intensity.

Some people appear to be very good at recognizing even brief facial affect displays. It is a very useful skill in some professional roles: bank loan officers, psychiatrists, nurses, police officers. Some people in these roles, either through training or because they were talented to begin with, demonstrate excellent ability to recognize expressions. Even good observers, however, may "block" on some emotion. They may have difficulty recognizing anger, or disgust, or happiness. This blocking is particularly evident with people who have emotional disorders. Increasingly, it appears that different emotional problems may be diagnosed by the way in which the patient can identify and express, on request, the primary affects. Finally, individuals in different toxic states show impaired abilities to recognize affect. The toxic states differ, however, and the individual on marijuana appears to pick up a different range of affects than the man on alcohol.

Other Facial Signs

So far we have largely talked about the relatively involuntary expressions of emotion, the facial displays that well up, modified only by the culturally learned "display rules." But the individual can also create an apparent expression of emotion, even when no affect is present. And the face can be used to produce other signs.

The "put-on" expression of emotion may be done either (a) with the expectation (or hope) that the receiver will take it for a felt affect, or (b) with the open indication that it is an act. An example of the first would be a young lad who puts on an angry face hoping to scare off a bully. (As indicated before, if such an expression covers up some other emotion, such as fear, it is called "masking." If no other emotion is present, it does not "mask" another affect; it simulates one which is not there.)

Just as some people are good at catching expressions of emotion generally, some individuals are very adept at ferreting out simulated as opposed to felt affects. Among the cues that people may use are inconsistencies in (a) partials, (b) blends, and (c) timing. The person who is simulating an affect display, may, for example, get part of the expression but not all of it. He may smile with his lips, but his eyes may be "icy cold," as the detective novels like to say. Second, the individual attempting simulation may get part of the affect he wants—but blend in another affect expression. He may smile in apparent pleasure, but his brows may knit in concern. Finally, the timing of the expression may be off. The person wants to display pleasure . . . and he does. But the reaction is a bit delayed, a beat off. It becomes apparent that the expression was not automatic; the individual had to think about the expression he wanted to display and then produce it. Similarly, the put-on expression may not last as long as it should. We sometimes see someone who appears to be happy in interaction. But the instant he turns his back, the signs of pleasure disappear. There are no lingering, slowly dissolving remnants of the earlier state. It is rather as if a mask has been dropped. We have been witnessing a "social smile"—rather than a felt affect.

Sometimes, of course, an individual puts on a face with no attempt at deception. He is, for example, reenacting an emotion felt earlier. He says, "So that made me feel just terrible"—and he re-creates his sad expression. Or, an individual may be imitating the affect display of someone else: "She looked like the cat that ate a canary"—followed by a broad grin. Some are very good at mimicking the expressions of others. They can visually re-create images of their own joy, or excitement, or horror. They spice their conversations or enliven their speeches with appropriate facial gestures. And we tend to think of these individuals as "vivacious," "expressive," and "dynamic"—rather than as "deadpan" or "boring."

While the expressions of emotion, felt or simulated, provide the basic vocabulary of facial communication, the human face can telegraph a wide spectrum of subtle but telling statements. An individual may look serious or kidding, concerned or indifferent, seductive or hostile. The communicator may indicate that he is believing or skeptical, accepting or unaccepting, sincere or insincere. These cues may, in turn, have an impact on the relationship, on the ongoing communication system.

In another area of regulation, certain facial expressions may be linked to particular phases of a communication system. Evidence now suggests, for example, that the eyebrow "flash," the rapid raising and lowering of the brow, may be a universal form of greeting.[7] Finally, the head and face may be used as a pointer or indicator. In some cultures, for example, it is impolite to point with one's finger. Rather, pointing is done with the lips or with a head movement. A similar "pointer" is simply the way the head is turned, and the way gaze is directed.

EYE BEHAVIOR

The eye is poetically referred to as "the window to the soul." As a chief sensory receptor, which is easily observable by another, it can reveal much. It is likely to signal what interests. It also may indicate what is being

[7] I. Eibl-Eibesfeldt, "Similarities and Differences Between Cultures in Expressive Movements," in Robert A. Hinde (ed.), Non-verbal Communication (New York: Cambridge University Press, 1972), pp. 297–314.

rejected. In interaction, it appears to signal major shifts in the pattern of communication. Like a traffic signal, it helps regulate the communication system.

At a physiological level, the eye dilates in darkness. The organ operates automatically to open its lens and receive more light. But dilation can also be caused by psychological factors. The presentation of interesting objects, even in normal light, will cause the eye to dilate. Both extremely pleasant stimuli, such as beautiful women or handsome men, and very unpleasant stimuli, such as spiders or snakes, may cause the eye to dilate. This fact has been used by researchers in the mass media. They have exposed viewers to ads and other messages. Then, with an eye camera, measurements are taken of eye movement and pupil dilation.[8]

Normally, dilation would not be under the control of the producer. He cannot easily use it as a sign for communication. There are, however, ancient drugs, such as belladonna, which have been used for centuries by women who wish to make their pupils larger and their eyes more alluring. Similarly, photographers have retouched photographs, widening the pupil, to make the woman more attractive. The observer who sees such a retouched photograph or an individual with drug-widened eyes usually knows something is different. Observers vary in their response, but typically, the actual cue is one of awareness. The observer cannot pinpoint what it is that makes the individual different.

 • Also at a basic physiological level, the eyes dilate during problem solving. And they tend to move either right or left. People can, in fact, be classified as "right-lookers" or "left-lookers." The average individual makes about 75 percent of his movements in one direction or the other. This "right-looking" and "left-looking," in turn, appears to be related to activities in the two cerebral hemispheres. Right-looking is related to left hemisphere activity, and left-looking is related to right hemisphere activity. The left hemisphere tends to be strong on verbal and digital processing, while the right hemisphere excels in the nonverbal, in analogic, and spatial problem solving. You may be able to sort the "verbals" from the "nonverbals" by asking questions that the individual works "in his head." (See Appendix B.)

From basic physiological findings, predictions have been made about eye behavior in social interaction. Perhaps, for example, gaze will increase toward individuals we like. And conversely, perhaps gaze will decrease toward those we dislike. Also at a fundamental information-processing level, perhaps eyes will be averted to avoid feedback. When the person doesn't want more information, or wants to think, he may close off incoming stimuli. These predictions do tend to be borne out, although

---

[8] E. H. Hess, "Attitude and Pupil Size," *Scientific American*, 212, April, 1965, pp. 46–54.

eye behavior in interaction turns out to be a complex and intricate pattern, a choreographed exchange that depends on the mutual activity of both partners.

In the formation of a communication system, eye contact is a crucial key. We try to "catch the eye" of the waiter so we can engage him in our service. At other times we are careful not to "catch the eye." As we walk down the street, we let our eyes rove with what Erving Goffman has called "civil inattention." We pass over the eyes of other people and don't pause with a look of recognition. Goffman points out that we usually exchange glances until we are about 8 feet from the other person.[9] Then we set ourselves on a noncollision course, and lower our eyes, a sort of "dimming of the lights."

In conversation, the speaker is likely to catch the listener's attention. But then, before launching into a long utterance, the speaker will drop his eyes. He will make periodic checks, to see if his listener is still there—and still a listener. But he will avoid eye contact at pauses when, for example, he is trying to think of how to complete his thought. When he is finished, however, he will return his gaze to the listener and prepare to give up the floor.

During an interaction, the participants look at each other between 25 to 75 percent of the time. This mutual looking tends to increase when the participants like each other, and when they are deeply involved in their discussion. As expected, eye contact can drop when touchy subjects are brought up. And people tend to have less eye contact when they are very close to each other physically. Moving across cultures, distinct differences can be seen in what is appropriate eye behavior. The British apparently "stare" more than we do. Meanwhile, in many cultures, it is polite to avert the eyes when conversing with a superior. The American's demand to "look me in the eye" is very dissonant to the foreigner who has been taught to communicate respect by doing just the opposite. The degree of eye contact may, in turn, follow a cultural pattern that prescribes touch–no touch, interpersonal spacing, and the way people orient their bodies (e.g., standing face to face versus shoulder to shoulder).[10]

HEAD NODS

The vertical head nod for affirmation, and the head shake for negation, were long thought to be human universals. Theories were developed about the origin of this gesture in man's repertoire. One suggested that the infant uses an up and down movement in searching for his mother's breast,

---

[9] Erving Goffman, *Behavior in Public Places* (New York: Free Press, 1963), p. 84.
[10] O. Michael Watson, *Proxemic Behavior: A Cross-Cultural Study* (The Hague: Mouton, 1970).

and a sidewise movement to get rid of the nipple when he is through feeding. There are, however, cultures that do not exhibit this same pattern of up and down movements to signal "yes."

Within our own culture, the head nod is seen as agreement, support, affirmation. Meanwhile, the head shake is seen as disagreement. Within the communication context, the head nod becomes a powerful reinforcer. When one participant nods, the other tends to increase whatever it is he's doing. In conversation, a series of slow head nods is likely to keep the speaker going indefinitely. Meanwhile, a series of fast head nods typically indicates that the listener now wants to speak. He wants the speaker to hurry up. He agrees. He knows. He is preparing to interrupt.

Beyond that, the pattern of the head nods becomes an intricate gestural dance, apparently related to events in the linguistic band, and to the behaviors of the other participant. While the pattern is elaborate, most people in the culture know it thoroughly. And if head nods are completely inhibited, interaction will slow down. It may terminate. Or the other participant may ask: "What's wrong?"

In summary, man produces many cues: cues of general facial appearance, cues of expression, cues of eye behavior, and cues of head movements. Some of these cues are enduring, difficult for the producer to change, but perhaps particularly informative for the observer. Some cues are semifixed, perhaps linked to a particular communication situation. And some are momentary—fleeting but telling cues in interaction. Some of these cues are used to encode content, such as the re-creation of an earlier expression, or the imitation of another's facial display. But many of these cues are in the area of regulation. They reveal inner emotional states. They reveal attempts to hide feelings, or fabricate feelings which are not felt.

The communicator may find these cues of the head and face particularly informative, in assessing the state of the interaction, what the other communicator is feeling, about himself, about his fellow communicators, about the communication situation. The communicator may find that his own facial cues can enliven, punctuate, regulate. He may be able to telegraph his own intentions and read the intentions of others. He may be able to assess the impact his messages are having. And he may increase their impact with his own facial cues.

DISCUSSION–EXERCISES

1. Examine facial expressions in news photos, ads, illustrations, and on television. What affects are being displayed? What are they being used to communicate?

2. In front of a mirror, try performing the following affect displays:

happiness, sadness, surprise, fear, anger, disgust. How good are you at producing affect displays? Are some of your affects more convincing than others?

3. As you watch movie and television dramas, consider the following: (a) What appearance cues are used in casting characters? (b) When one character is deceiving another character, what cues does the actor use to let the audience know that deception is going on? (Often, these cues are broadest in television situation comedies.) (c) What other kinds of facial expressions do actors use to communicate with their audience?

4. Experiment with eye contact. While walking down the street, keep looking at someone as he approaches. What does he do? In a conversation, increase or decrease your eye contact. What effect does this have?

5. Experiment with head nods. Try reinforcing someone with head nods. Then stop all head movements. What happens?

8

performance 3:
the hands and body

LEARNING TIPS

This chapter deals with the performance codes of the hands and body.
It is designed to

1. Introduce you to
    - cues arising from body appearance
    - cues arising from posture
    - signs produced by hand movements
    - the body as a receiver as well as a sender of signs

2. Review and expand on five types of hand gestures:
    - illustrators
    - regulators
    - adaptors
    - affect displays
    - emblems

3. Alert you to six types of illustrators:
    - pointers
    - pictographs
    - spatials
    - kinetographs
    - batons
    - ideographs

4. Introduce you to these additional concepts:
    - self-adaptors
    - alter-adaptors
    - object-adaptors
    - quasi-courtship behavior
    - points
    - positions
    - presentations

THOUGHT STARTERS

1. When you say that someone "talks with his hands," just what is it that his hands say?

2. If you really wanted to insult someone with a gesture, just what gesture would you use?

3. If you wanted to console someone, how would you touch him?

Bill was thinking that Al's hourglass hand gesture was very descriptive.

"How are we going to get there?" Xan asked.

"I thought we'd hitchhike," Bill replied.

"Oh."

MODERN MAN IS BODY CONSCIOUS. Fashions shift. The body, once wrapped like a cocoon, has emerged like a naked butterfly. The pendulum may swing again; but at the moment, fashion offers a rainbow of choice. The mind–body dualism that pervaded Western thought is being challenged. Increasingly, man accepts his body. He pursues sensory awareness. He diets. He exercises. He tries massage. He sunbathes. The female form is employed—and exploited—in the mass media. Ads are populated with youthful lithe figures. Clothing styles reveal, accentuate, and dramatize the human body.

In interaction, man also uses his body. He postures. He uses his hands. He leans forward. Or he turns away. He points. He pokes. His hands flow with the rhythm of his words. He touches. He strokes. He folds his arms. He crosses his legs. He moves toward. He moves away. He moves against.

This chapter explores man's body as a source of markers. It examines (a) body appearance cues, (b) posture, (c) hand movements, and (d) the body as a receiver of messages.

BODY APPEARANCE

Overall body appearance provides demographic data about sex, age, and race. In addition, it classifies according to cultural standards of beauty. The rolypoly Rubenesque model of yesteryear has given way to a more scrawny ideal type. Finally, body types are associated with personality and temperament. "Yon Cassius" is seen as having a "lean and hungry look." Meanwhile, dumpling-shaped men are seen as jolly.

Three major body types have been described: (a) the endomorph, who is round, fat, and soft; (b) the mesomorph, who is muscular, bony, and athletic; and (c) the ectomorph, who is thin, tall, and fragile. These body configurations have been correlated with temperament. And studies have explored the extent to which observers agree on the sign value of these body markers. To what extent can people make accurate predictions on the basis of these cues?

Observers tend to agree that the endormorph, the fat person, is good-natured and agreeable, talkative, and sympathetic. The mesomorph, the muscular individual, is seen as self-reliant, adventurous, and mature. Meanwhile, the skinny ectomorph is seen as tense, nervous, pessimistic, and quiet. Although many exceptions exist and few individuals fit the physique categories perfectly, these expectations lead to better than chance predictions. Data do suggest that endomorphs are affable, affectionate, and sympathetic. Mesomorphs tend to be energetic, adventurous, and competitive. And ectomorphs may be tense, thoughtful, and withdrawn.

These signs then have some predictive value. They are likely to influence decisions at the formation stage, when the communicator is weighing potential costs and rewards. Further, they may influence perceptions of source credibility: who is seen as competent, trustworthy, dynamic. Finally, a growing body of data suggests that sheer tallness may have important sign value in the communication context. Taller men get better job offers and better starting salaries and are preferred for executive positions.

POSTURE

The way a man walks and stands and sits is frequently taken as a message about himself. These cues are read for self-confidence, for signs of energy or fatigue, for clues about status. In interactions, man orients himself toward others. He can stand over another, or kneel in front of him. He can face him directly, or "give him the shoulder." He can lean forward, or recline backward. He can lean to the right or the left. He can sit erect or he can slouch. He can fold his arms and legs in a tight, defensive posture, or he can "open up" in a sprawling, relaxed pose. He can adopt the same pose as his fellow communicator, or he can take a contrary posture.

Moving across cultures, sharp differences are seen in postural demands exacted during interaction. In many cultures, one bows before an elder.

One sits at the feet of a superior. One may be required to face an important person, and avoid turning the back. In our own culture, similar but more subtle cues have been noticed in the signaling of status. Superiors are able to take more relaxed positions than their inferiors. On the other hand, when someone moves to take charge of a meeting, he sits erect. When tension rises at a meeting, those holding the same view may adopt similar postures. In the formation and regulation of interactions, postural cues tend to be seen as signs: symptoms reflecting the participant's inner state and signals about the emerging group structure.

HAND MOVEMENTS

In the 1930s several Nazi theorists developed arguments supporting the notion of a master race. One suggested that man could be divided into four major races: Nordic man, Western man, Eastern man, and Mediterranean man. Nordic man was seen as energetic, mature, and capable of great achievement. Western man, which included the American, was, on the other hand, child-like, simple, and playful. A related theory of the time suggested that races could be distinguished by their gestures. The Jewish "race," for example, was seen to have uniquely Jewish gestures as part of their inborn qualities. This theory suggested that Jews could be spotted by their hand gestures, even when they had only a little Jewish blood.

This spurred anthropologist Franz Boas and his colleagues at Columbia University to study man's gestural patterns. David Efron, a Boaz student, examined gestures on the Lower East Side of New York, among immigrants from Southern Italy and Jewish immigrants from Eastern Europe.[1] Efron found that indeed he could discriminate differences among first-generation immigrants. The Italians used broad, full-arm gestures while the Jewish immigrants tended to use movements close to the body, movements that seemed to trace the flow of what was being said. Efron also found, however, that among the second generation, these unique gestural patterns began to fade. Italian youngsters were picking up Jewish gestures, and vice versa. Unfortunately, with the outbreak of World War II, Efron returned to his native Argentina, and he has only recently returned to studying man's gestural codes.

Recently, however, Efron's work has been picked up by Paul Ekman and Wallace Friesen. His original scheme for classifying gestures has been incorporated into the distinctions of emblems, illustrators, regulators, adaptors, and affect displays. We first introduced these categories in Chap-

---

[1] David Efron, *Gesture and Environment* (New York: King's Crown, 1941); republished as *Gesture, Race, and Culture* (The Hague: Mouton, 1972).

ter 6, in discussing the performance codes generally. Now let's take a closer look, with special attention to hand movements.

Illustrators

As noted earlier, illustrators comment and elaborate on messages in the verbal band. Illustrators are done primarily with the hands, but they can also be done with the head, the face, and the total body. At least six types of illustrator have been distinguished: (a) pointers, (b) pictographs, (c) spatials, (d) kinetographs, (e) batons, and (f) ideographs. The *pointer* simply points to some present object. "I want that one." (Finger point, head nod, pointing with the chin or lips.) The *pictograph* draws a picture of an object in the air. "She looks like this." (Hands make curved hourglass.) The *spatials* show size or relationship. "It was just this big." (Hands held appropriate distance apart.) The *kinetographs* recreate some bodily action. "So I hit him." (Fist swings through air.) The *batons* are movements which accentuate or punctuate. They beat out the tempo of the verbal statement. "I really (gesture) mean it (gesture)!" Finally, the *ideographs* trace the flow of an idea. They tend to be rolling or flowing movements that help the receiver see the connection between ideas or the direction a line of thought is moving. "It's nice, but on the other hand. . . ." (Gesture moves in one direction, then back toward the other side.)

In interaction, the pointers help clarify ambiguities in the verbal band, or they can add emphasis. A word such as "you" can be a specific individual, or it can mean the general "you all." A pointer, directed at you, the individual, clears up this verbal ambiguity. The baton, when done with a rhythmic chopping motion, is usually a sign of emphasis. On the other hand, a single baton, or an arhythmic series of batons, usually is a sign of punctuation and division. "We must consider Al (chop) and Bill (chop) and Xan (chop)." This suggests that we will consider each of three individuals. Or: "We must consider Al and Bill (chop) and Xan (chop)." Or: "We must consider Al (chop) and Bill and Xan (chop)." We are going to consider three people, but the baton tells us whether we are going to consider each individually, or Al and Bill together and then Xan, or Al as opposed to Bill and Xan.

Among the ideographs, a slow circular motion is likely to mean "more than the specific words I have used," that is, this is just one example of the larger phenomenon I mean. Palm orientation may relate to the speaker's degree of certainty (Figure 8-1). Statements accompanied by a palm-up gesture are likely to be qualified, as if the speaker were saying, "I think," or "It seems to me." Meanwhile, a palm-down gesture is the equivalent of saying "clearly" or "certainly."

FIGURE 8-1 Illustrating.

Try saying this phrase while making the illustrated hand movements:
"Just let me say . . ."

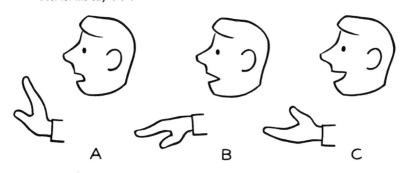

With the hand held up (A) the message is likely to be: "Wait, let me say. . . ."
With the palm down (B), the message is more likely to imply: "Now let me tell
you how it really is. . . ." With the palm up, the underlying message may
be: "Well, just let me say I think that . . ." Or: "It seems to me . . ."

In general, the illustrator can introduce redundancy by providing in
the nonverbal band added emphasis for what is being transmitted in the
verbal band. The illustrator may also clarify, reducing uncertainties that
might arise with ambiguous words and references. Finally, the illustrator
can indicate the speaker's relationship to his verbal output, how he
feels about it in relationship to his listener.

As Efron learned, patterns of illustration appear to be learned in the
family, which in turn absorbs the larger cultural pattern. People illustrate
more when they are excited or involved with their ideas. They illustrate
even when they are alone, talking on a telephone or over an intercom. In
these situations, illustrators drop off sharply, however, and it appears that
the communicator performs the illustrators with the expectation that
they will aid his receiver.

Regulators

Regulators are nonverbal behaviors which control the interaction.
They indicate when a speaker is about to give up the floor, when someone
else may speak, when someone else *must* speak. The listener, in turn,
regulates by giving reinforcement, and by signaling his desires to speak or
not speak. Perhaps the most important regulators reside in the head area,
in nods, smiles, and eye contact. But regulation does also occur with the

hands and body. The hand extended out, palm toward the listener, says: Wait, let me speak. Or: Don't interrupt me. Or: I'm going to say it anyway.

Albert Scheflen suggests that interaction is organized into units, not unlike the paragraph, the chapter, the whole book.[2] This organizing is accomplished with three types of regulators: (a) *points*, (b) *positions*, and (c) *presentations*. The points occur every few sentences. Primarily done with the head, neck, and eyes, they indicate the end of a structural unit, the grouping of an integrated set of thoughts. They appear to aid the listener pull together and comprehend the last few sentences. The position is a larger unit, comparing several points. It corresponds to a point of view taken in a conversation. Body posture and interpersonal space help mark off these positions. Finally, the presentation incorporates the total set of movements in an interaction. With a major shift in posture, the participant signals withdrawl, at least temporarily, from the scene of interaction.

In his analyses of therapists and clients, Scheflen has observed interesting patterns of interaction, including what he calls "quasi-courtship" behavior. This includes preening behavior, such as straightening the tie, pulling up the socks, patting the hair. And it includes subtle movements of flirtation, eye contact, gesture, and body posture.

In one of his examples, a complex set of regulators operate among a therapist, a client, and the client's family. The mother leans forward to talk to the therapist and engages in quasi-courtship behavior. The father then taps his foot. The grandmother and the daughter, who are sitting on either side of the mother, then cross their legs toward each other, creating a protective barrier in front of the mother. The mother then stops talking to the therapist and leans back. This pattern occurs again and again in the interaction. Scheflen sees this as a code system of regulation that has been learned by this family group.[3]

Regulators appear to be learned within a culture, and perhaps, as in the above case, within family or other groupings. When an individual moves into another culture, he may find some difficulties in adjusting to other patterns of regulation. And he may not be able to identify what it is that is different. In our culture, for example, certain pauses or silences are the cue for the other person to begin speaking. In other cultures, a similar pause may not have the same significance, and the speaker will feel he's being impolitely interrupted if the listener *does* begin to speak.

[2] Albert Scheflen, *Body Language and the Social Order* (Englewood Cliffs, N.J.: Prentice-Hall, 1972).

[3] An alternative explanation, based on pure learning, is proposed by Morton Wiener, Shannon Devoe, Stuart Rubinow, and Jesse Geller, "Nonverbal Behavior and Nonverbal Communication," *Psychological Review*, 79, 1972, pp. 185–214.

Adaptors

Adaptors are behaviors which once served a useful purpose, but which now are part of the individual's habit repertoire. They may no longer serve their original purpose. And they may be performed in a truncated form. Three types have been distinguished: (a) *self-adaptors*, (b) *alter-adaptors*, and (c) *object-adaptors*. The self-adaptors involve self-touch, soothing, scratching, biting, cradling some part of the body. Alter-adaptors involve another person: touching, kissing, nuzzling, holding. Object-adaptors make use of some artifact in the environment. The object is played with, stroked, punched, wielded.

In interaction, self-adaptors may be very revealing of the individual's feelings about the situation, about the others around him. He may, for example, put his hand over his mouth, as he would to prevent himself from speaking. He may wipe himself around the eyes, a gesture which was originally associated with wiping tears in grief. He may cover his eyes, as if to ward off unpleasant stimuli. He may pick and scratch at himself, in a modified form of self-attack. Or, he may rub and massage himself, as if giving reassurance and support.

The adaptor is typically done without awareness. And the particular gesture is learned within the individual's own experience. Interpretation of adaptors then becomes a very speculative endeavor. They do emerge as important signs, however, in communication systems of long running. A husband and wife, for example, may over time develop strong hypotheses about the meanings of specific adaptors for each other. Similarly, a psychiatrist over time is likely to develop distinct interpretations for adaptors he sees in different types of distress, and for the adaptors of a particular patient.

Affect Displays

Affect displays are those presentations of emotion, primarily seen in the face, but also evident in hand movements and body posture. The recent work of Paul Ekman and Wallace Friesen on deception suggests that the face may be the best expressor of emotion, followed by the hands, and then the total body. From the face, specific categories of emotion can be determined: happiness, sadness, anger, surprise, fear, or disgust. While from the rest of the body, affect tone can most easily be sorted into positive and negative (i.e., pleasant or unpleasant). In trying to deceive another person, however, most control may be exercised on the face, with succeedingly less control demonstrated in hands and body. This means that the face may be most expressive. But it is also the best liar. The hands and feet do not "talk" as much. But they tell the truth. Similar speculation has centered on the difference between right-handed and left-handed gestures. The left hand is controlled by the right hemisphere of the brain, which is more analogic. Meanwhile, the right hand is controlled by the left hemisphere which is more digital and analytic. Thus right-handed gestures may be more closely coordinated to verbal output, while left-handed gestures may be more revealing of "feelings" and hence "more honest."

Emblems

Emblems are gestures that can replace a word or phrase. They stand alone, or they can mesh with a particular phrase. They are learned within a culture, and may be specific to that culture. Finally, they tend to be performed with intent and awareness. Some are coded iconically. They resemble their referent. Or, they have generalized from a recognizable act. Drawing a finger across the throat, for example, symbolizes slitting one's neck. It is used to mean: "finished." Or, in radio and television studios, it means: "cut it off," or "end it."

Some emblems have a complicated history and in their present form seem quite arbitrary for their referent. The two-finger peace gesture grew out of the World War II "V" gesture. The fingers stood for the letter "V," which in turn stood for "Victory." Similarly, in the A-Okay sign, the circle created by the fingers stood for the "O" in "O.K." Meanwhile, O.K. means "all right" or "good." And why? It came into American jargon in the 1840 presidential election. Martin Van Buren was the Democratic candidate, and he was born in Old Kinderhook, New York. In New York City, the Democratic O.K. Club was formed to support Van Buren. This group in turn became a powerful political influence; to run for office, or be appointed to office, you had to get its "O.K."

Obviously, in a culture which does not speak English, and one which does not share American political history, the O-shaped fingers might have another meaning. That same gesture does, in fact, have a different, and obscene, meaning in many cultures. It is a gesture representing the female genitalia. If the gesture is done to a woman, it is a sexual proposal. If done to a man, it is casting aspersions on his masculinity. In either case, it is likely to be received as something less than an "O.K." gesture.

Because they originate within cultures, emblems may cause particular difficulties to the international traveler. The meaning he has for a gesture may not be shared by his host country. Soviet leaders, when appearing in this country, frequently make a common Russian gesture, the clasped hands held over the head. To the American, of course, this is the sign used by a boxer who has won. The Russian, meanwhile, makes that gesture in recognition of the tribute being paid him. He is not commenting, at least publicly, on the meetings he has just had with the American head of state.

Emblems often occur in situations where the verbal band is fully used or blocked. The radio and television director, for example, has a set of emblems he can use in silence on stage, or through a sound-proofed glass partition. Similarly, the flag waver on the flight deck of an aircraft carrier—or the mechanic motioning you onto the hoist—replaces verbalizations with gestures. Most sporting events have gestures for the officials, so their calls are unmistakable even above crowd noises. The baseball coach, meanwhile, has an elaborate set of signs that he uses to advise players. He may go through a seemingly random set of behaviors: touching the brim of his cap, hitching up his trousers, patting his chest, and so on, but some of these movements have significance (e.g., steal home). The sign system is complicated in that there is usually a preparatory signal. One gesture is performed that says: now, I mean for you to really do what this next gesture says. That is, one gesture is a signal which warns that the next gesture is a symbol, not a random movement. The coach, of course, could not have called his instructions across the field. Not only are the distances great, but the other team would overhear.

In each culture, sets of emblems seem to be associated with the formation stage and with the termination ritual. The European–American handshake is found in metropolitan centers around the world. But usage may vary slightly. In many Latin American countries, women shake hands when introduced to men. In the North American culture, the female-to-male handshake is optional and usually not performed except in very formal situations such as an official reception.

This form of handshake was not common in Ethiopia prior to World War II. Then it began to diffuse, first in the major centers, and then out into the countryside. It replaced a gesture in which the right arm was brought across the chest, done with an accompanying bow. In recent years, the cultural tradition was revived and a second wave of diffusion took place. Now the "European" handshake has been replaced in urban centers of Ethiopia, but it can still be found in rural backwaters.

In other areas a handshake, not necessarily of European origin, is part of a larger greeting pattern. In Nigeria, for example, one greeting starts with a very typical handshake. But then the thumbs are grasped. And finally, the hands are separated with a snapping of the fingers of the other person's hand. While all of this is going on, the subordinate in the interaction is making a slight bow, bending one knee and lowering his head in deference to the higher status or elder person.

Most cultures also appear to have obscene gestures, motions which can be hurled at an enemy from afar (see Figure 8-2). Typically, some phallic symbolism is involved, but the exact motion can vary. The common expression "I don't give a fig for him" appears to relate to an emblem which is not now popular in the American culture. The "fig" involves

непристойный

FIGURE 8-2   Which Is the Obscene Gesture?

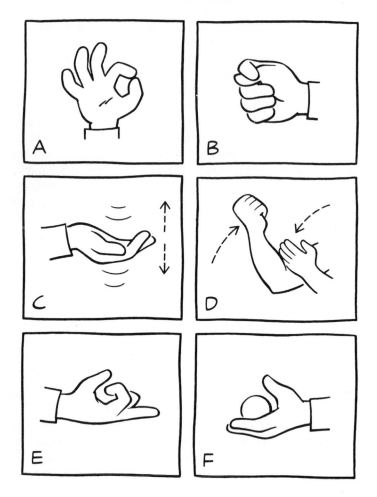

Actually, all these are obscene or taboo somewhere in the world. A is "A-OK" for the American, but not for many others. (See the text.) B is "the fig," a phallic symbol in some cultures. C, D, and E are variations, all with phallic connotations. In the United States, "the finger" (E) is delivered with a vertical thrust into the air; however, in many cultures the middle finger is pointed toward the target of insult. F represents the "left-hand taboo." In many cultures it is an insult to offer anything with the left hand since the left hand is reserved for cleansing oneself.

displaying the thumb between the first two fingers of a clenched fist. It is comparable in some parts of the world to "the finger" or "the arm."

In summary, man's hand movements provide a rich source of signs, as emblems, as illustrators, as regulators, as adaptors, and, to a lesser degree, as affect displays. The emblems tend to be markers that are produced with sign intent. They are clearly understood within a culture, but can cause problems for cross-cultural communicators. Illustrators similarly differ by culture. Pointing may be impolite, or it may be impolite with certain parts of the body. Similarly, it may be taboo to offer something with the left hand. Even pictographs and spatials may differ from society to society. In our culture, when we give the height of something we say "so high," holding the hand out, palm down. In some cultures that is appropriate for indicating the height of cattle, but when referring to humans the hand is held with its edge to the ground. The American elicits laughter when he says his daughter is "so high," and then measures her like a calf. Other cultures have still different ways of expressing the concept of "so high." In some African cultures the hand is held palm down when indicating the height of an adult—but palm up if the referent is a still-growing child. And in some Central American societies a child's height is given with the hand held palm toward the listener. The height is marked by the top of the fingertips.

THE BODY AS A SIGN RECEIVER

Lawrence Frank argued that a culture's social relationships are learned through touch: the handshake, holding, kissing, hugging, and so on.[4] He and others have suggested that the child learns to relate to another human being first through touch.[5] These patterns of interaction in turn undergird all the later patterns of interaction in life. In recent years, people interested in growth and therapy have explored touch as a means of making individuals aware of themselves and others.[6] Methods have been used to literally put one "in touch" with oneself and other humans.

In general, American culture tends to be a low-contact culture. This was noted by Sidney Jourard one day while sitting in a coffeehouse in San Juan, Puerto Rico.[7] There, a young couple might touch almost two

---

[4] Lawrence K. Frank, "Tactile Communication," *Genetic Psychology Monographs*, 56, 1957, pp. 123–155.

[5] M. F. A. Montagu, *Touching: The Human Significance of the Skin* (New York: Columbia University Press, 1971).

[6] Jane Howard, *Please Touch* (New York: Dell, 1970); see also William Schutz, *Joy* (New York: Grove Press, 1967).

[7] Sidney M. Jourard, "An Exploratory Study of Body-Accessibility," *British Journal of Social and Clinical Psychology*, 5, 1966, pp. 221–231.

hundred times in an hour. In this country, a similar couple might touch a couple of times. In Paris Jourard discovered that the French were less touch oriented than the Puerto Ricans, but the touch count there was over one hundred. Meanwhile, the British are even less touchable than Americans. They touch not at all during a typical hour. Figure 8-3 shows a chart that Jourard developed to explore touch behavior. He asked individuals where they had been touched, in the previous 12 months, by (a) their mother, (b) their father, (c) their closest friend of the opposite sex, and (d) their closest friend of the same sex.

He found sharp differences between the sexes, and clear differences on who touched whom where. Both men and women reported a high degree of hand contact with parents and friends but considerably less contact with other parts of the body. Among the pairs, male friends engage in lots of touch, particularly above the waist. The pair with least contact is father and daughter. See Appendix C for complete data.

FIGURE 8-3   Touch Chart: Where Do You Get Touched?

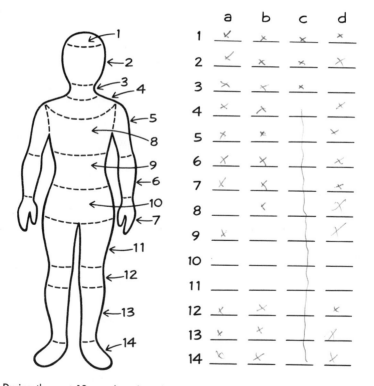

During the past 12 months, where have you been touched by (a) your mother, (b) your father, (c) your closest friend of the opposite sex, (d) your closest friend of the same sex? See Appendix C for comparative data.

Recently other researchers have suggested that the skin could be a good sign receptor, particularly when other sensory channels are impaired or overloaded. Frank Geldard has worked out an "optohapt alphabet" which can be communicated through the skin, using vibrators in nine locations.[8] Such schemes have been suggested, for example, to communicate to astronauts, who have their visual and auditory channels crammed. (Another suggestion has been to have scented capsules that give off warning odors in case of different malfunctions.)

Inventors are also now working on an electronic device which would allow a blind person to "see" with his skin.[9] A small television camera is mounted on the head and it transmits a pattern of sensations to the back. The skin of the back becomes, in effect, a television screen on which the environment is printed. The picture may not be great art, but it would permit the blind person to walk down the street without colliding with objects.

SUMMARY

This chapter has examined the human body as a sign producer and as a sign receiver. Overall appearance is likely to be read by observers for cues of sex, age, race, temperament. These markers may be important indicators in launching an interaction or in assessing qualifications and credibility. Similarly, posture may be looked to for signs of self-image, status, and orientation to others.

Hand movements present a rich store of markers which perform a variety of important functions. In particular, we discussed (a) emblems, (b) illustrators, (c) affect displays, (d) adaptors, and (e) regulators. Among the illustrators, some show size, some trace the flow of ideas and emphasize important points. In all, six types of illustrators have been distinguished: (a) pointers, (b) spatials, (c) ideographs, (d) batons, (e) kinetographs, and (f) pictographs. Similarly, the other classes of hand movements have subcategories. Adaptors, for example, may be self-adaptors, alter-adaptors, or object-adaptors. And regulators may be classed into points, positions, and presentations. Finally, the body can also act as a receiver of signs. And these messages of touch may play a profound role in shaping interaction—and perhaps in shaping human personality.

[8] Frank A. Geldard, "Body English," *Psychology Today*, 2, Dec. 1968, pp. 42–47.
[9] Benjamin W. White, Frank A. Saunders, Lawrence Seadden, Paul Bach-Y-Rita, and Carter C. Collins, "Seeing with the Skin," *Perception and Psychophysics*, 7, 1970, pp. 23–27.

DISCUSSION—EXERCISES

1. Take a well-illustrated magazine and examine the cartoons and the ads. What body appearance cues are used to communicate messages? What postures are used? What kinds of hand gestures are being used by the cartoon characters or the ad models?

2. Try to catch a speaker on television (e.g., a presidential address or press conference, a news clip of someone delivering a speech). Categorize the illustrators being used.

3. Engage a friend in conversation on a topic of considerable interest. Then watch the hand movements. What seems to lead to an increase in gesturing? Excitement? Difficulty getting a point across? Difficulty thinking of what to say or how to say it?

4. Make a list of all the emblems you can think of. How does your list compare with others'?

5. Experiment with touch. What happens when you increase your touch behavior?

9

time, space, and object

LEARNING TIPS

This chapter deals with artifactual codes and spatio-temporal codes. It is designed to

1. Alert you to (a) personal artifacts, (b) shared artifacts, and (c) public artifacts.

2. Introduce you to *proxemics* and these related concepts:
   - fixed-feature space
   - semi-fixed-feature space
   - informal space
   - intimate zone
   - casual-personal zone
   - social-consultative zone
   - public zone
   - axis
   - sociopetal
   - sociofugal

3. Introduce you to the following terms related to time:
   - informal time
   - formal time
   - technical time
   - monochronistic

THOUGHT STARTERS

1. What can you tell about an individual from observing his apparel? How confident are you of your inferences?

2. How close do you stand to a friend during conversation?

3. How late can you be for an appointment without giving an apology or an explanation?

"Are you sure we're in the right place?"
"It looks like the place."
"Maybe we're just early."
"Yeah."

TIME TALKS. SPACE SPEAKS. ARTIFACTS ARTICULATE. Places proclaim. And perhaps objects object. So is the claim of Sherlock Holmes. So is the observation of psychiatrists, psychologists, and anthropologists, who see elaborate messages in man's use of time, space, and object.

The way man arranges himself in time and space can have sign value for the astute observer. The way man creates, selects, arranges, and presents his artifacts may reveal much about his intentions, feelings, and aspirations. Often, this use of time, space, and object is done without an intent to communicate. It is a symptom, a signal, an index. But the aware communicator can use time, space, and artifact in the purposeful creation of signs. He can use these code systems to structure communication situations, to facilitate or inhibit interaction, to maintain and perpetuate effective communication systems. This chapter explores man's use of time, space, and artifact. It examines the markers that can be created, and the sign values that can be generated.

THE ARTIFACTUAL CODES

Man surrounds himself with tools and props. They often have a utilitarian function. But even the most mundane objects are likely to be decorated. They are likely to serve as decoration in a larger context. They become expressions of man's taste, of his image of himself, of his status, and his aspirations.

Compared to the performance codes, the artifactual codes may be (a) less intentional, (b) slower fading, and (c) more impersonal. While the manipulation of a status symbol may be done with great awareness and intent, most artifactual displays serve a double purpose: (a) they are useful in themselves (e.g., clothing keeps off the weather), and (b) they are decorations or expressions. Both the use and expression may have sign value for an observer. We know from his stethoscope that the man is a doctor; we know from the *way* he uses his stethoscope that he is competent or incompetent, gentle or brutal. The decoder must make an additional estimate of the extent to which the producer has purposefully manipulated his artifacts with intent, whether they are symptoms, signals, or symbols.

Among performance codes, many are "rapid-fading" signs. Speech, sounds, and movements are produced and then they disappear. As a communication code this is very efficient. It leaves the channel open for succeeding messages. It does not, of course, allow for storage and replay. One of the key functions of the mediatory codes is to capture, on paper, film, or tape, the otherwise fast-fading messages. With the artifactual code, the object (and its placement) is not fast-fading. It tends to stay in place and continues to send its message throughout an interaction. If for example, a man is in formal wear, he cannot, like Clark Kent, swiftly change costumes when new messages are required. He may, of course, be able to signal a shift in presentation by becoming less formal. He may take off his coat, loosen his tie, unbutton his collar, take off his shoes.

The longevity of the artifact also means that it continues as a marker even when its creator or arranger has left. The artifact may be a "to whom it may concern" message from an anonymous source. I walk into an empty office and I make inferences about the person who works there, on the basis of his artifacts and the way they are arranged. At one time, I owned a Frank Lloyd Wright house. That was a very powerful artifactual sign which continued to "tell me" things about the architect though he was long dead. My choice of such a house, in turn, said "something" about me; visitors learned things about me even if I wasn't home.

Personal Artifacts

Some artifacts, such as clothing and personal effects, are carried with the individual. Their choice and presentation is typically seen as reflecting that person's inner states. Clothing, at least traditionally, was an obvious cue to the sex of the wearer. Similarly, clothing styles are sharply age-graded. There are garments which are appropriate for young girls which are not worn by old ladies, and vice versa. In addition, clothing is often read as a cue of status and even occupation. Status cues include the expense of the garment, its age and condition, the degree to which it is high fashion or out of style. Some clothing artifacts become the symbol for occupational groups: hard-hats, jocks, blue-collar workers, white-collar workers.

Clothing is also seen as reflecting the personality, attitudes, and values of the wearer. Some people have a strong interest in clothes. Others are indifferent. Some are concerned primarily with economy in their dress. Others emphasize comfort. Still others reflect a concern with conformity. And some use clothing for decoration and self-expression. Modern T-shirts, with a vast array of printed verbal and nonverbal symbols, have become a new communication channel between the wearer and the world.

The most intentional use of clothing as communication is in uniforms. Individuals in different roles are dressed differently, prestructuring the interactions they will have. The uniform indicates status, appropriate communication content, appropriate rules of interchange. On many campuses, moves have been made to take the campus police out of uniform. But these attempts have been resisted, sometimes for surprising reasons.

At one large midwestern university, police were taken out of their uniforms. Their weapons were removed. They were dressed instead in blue blazers with a crest on the coat pocket. One immediate result was a morale problem on the police force. Many of the men simply quit. The uniform was an important part of their self-image. Their chief advanced several reasons for having the men back in uniform. He argued that without the uniform, people who needed help had a harder time finding a policeman. Second, he argued that the uniform was a symbol of authority which could stop trouble before it started. The uniform, he argued, would inhibit law breaking. Burglaries would be prevented. Fights could be stopped more easily. Potential rioters would think twice before taking destructive action. The chief also argued that the uniform made the officer impersonal. He could do his job more objectively. People responded to the uniform, not the man. Finally, the chief said he wanted his men in uniform because when there was trouble he wanted them to stand their ground. In case of a riot or a difficult situation, he didn't want them fading into the crowd. He wanted them to play their role, no matter how tough it might get. Somewhat surprisingly, the chief got support from some normally opposing forces. They, too, wanted the officers in uniform so they could be spotted. They didn't want policemen skulking around in "plain clothes."

Shared Artifacts

Larger, semimovable objects are frequently shared by more than one person. They may play an important role in structuring the interaction.

They may put up barriers. They may enclose the communicators. They may enforce status: for example, the man sitting behind a desk. They may also serve as a "conversation piece," an artifact which makes the formation stage of interaction easier.

Franklin Roosevelt had a desk covered with small artifacts, mementos picked up on his travels, gifts people had given him, and so on. He could always put a visitor at ease by commenting on some object that would fascinate the caller. Meanwhile, one executive recently had his office stripped of fine, modern oil paintings. He found they were too much of a conversation piece. Visitors would get absorbed in discussing art and would not get down to business. The trend today is toward executive desks which are free of artifacts, save perhaps one or two that are either very functional or very expressive of the individual. Meanwhile, the executive is likely to have a "conversation area" where he can move for certain types of interaction. He gets out from behind his desk and chats with his visitors seated in easy chairs around a coffee table.

Public Artifacts

Some artifacts are shared by many: meeting areas, whole rooms, buildings, monuments, and other architectural structures. The richness of the facility is likely to be read as a sign of the owner's status and influence. Important men have important offices. They live in impressive homes, in smart suburbs. Important corporations have modern, large buildings in good locations. And big governments have awesome public buildings, monumental monuments, impressive embassies.

Within these artifacts, many cues are set to direct traffic, to prescribe behavior, to proscribe admittance to "backstage" areas. These cues may be very effective determiners of the kind of human interaction which can and will take place. They may determine who will interact with whom, and what they will interact about. They may determine the kind of interaction, either formal or informal, tense or relaxed, pleasant or unpleasant. The interrogation room of a prison, for example, is likely to be different from the executive cocktail lounge.

In quite a different dimension, some artifacts have shared and public meaning for a large group. They are symbols rather than mere signals. A flag, for example, is an artifact which is used by all within a nation. When it is used inappropriately as a personal artifact, sanctions are involved. And they can be severe. During World War I, for example, a mob tried to force a man of German extraction to kiss the American flag. He objected that Old Glory was "nothing but a piece of cotton with paint on it" and that it might be covered with germs. The case ended up in court in Butte, Montana, and under the flag-desecration laws, the man was sentenced to 10 to 20 years imprisonment at hard labor. In recent years, a number of court cases have resulted from people wearing the flag, flying it upside down to protest government actions, and so on.

In summary, artifacts can be used to produce a variety of signs. Some, like flags and trophies, are symbols, very similar to gestural emblems. They are produced with intent and elicit shared public understanding. Some, such as dark mourning clothes or a black armband, are like affect displays; they are symptoms of a particular state. And many are like illustrators or regulators, signaling who is in and out of interaction, indexing various communication activities, determining how the participants will play their respective communication roles.

MESSAGES OF SPACE

Space can communicate messages of status. That which is more important is accorded more space. And it is placed higher than less important elements. The important man has a big office, high up in the corporate building. The town's tycoon has the big house on top of the hill. The important message is presented with a lot of white space around it. It is placed near the top of the page. In addition, cues of space can influence interaction. Interpersonal distance, for example, has been seen as a cue of liking or disliking, trust or distrust, discussion of personal subject matter or public topic.

Edward Hall has coined the word *proxemics* for "the study of the ways in which man gains knowledge of the content of other men's minds through judgments of behavior patterns associated with varying degrees of proximity between them." [1] He has explored the sign value of space use for the individual, the group, and the larger society.[2]

Circles of Space

Hall distinguishes three types of space: (a) fixed-feature space, the type created by immovable walls and objects; (b) semi-fixed-feature space, created by large objects such as chairs and tables; and (c) informal space, the bubble of personal space individuals carry with them as they move from interaction to interaction. For the individual, his informal space is divided into regions. Within each ring, certain types of interaction can take place. Certain types of content can be dealt with. Nearest to the

---

[1] Edward T. Hall, "Silent Assumptions in Social Communication," *Disorders of Communication*, 42, 1964, pp. 41–55.
[2] Edward T. Hall, *The Hidden Dimension* (New York: Doubleday, 1966).

individual is "intimate" space, ranging from contact to about 18 inches. This is the zone for handling secrets and whispered confidences. Next is the "casual-personal" zone, ranging from 1½ to 4 feet. This is the region for normal personal interaction. From 4 feet to about 12 feet is the "social-consultative" zone. This is the area for handling impersonal business. This is the man seated behind a desk conversing with a visitor. Finally, is the "public" zone, from 12 feet out to the limits of hearing. This is the region of the public speaker, addressing a mass audience.

. Hall's zones are drawn for the middle-class American, particularly those living in the Northeast. But each culture has its own zoning, its own partitioning of space for communication purposes. Even within the United States, the use of space differs by region, by social class, by ethnic background. In many parts of the world, the interpersonal distance for "casual" conversation overlaps the American's "intimate" zone. The man from another culture may feel completely comfortable at a close range which will make the American squirm. Standing in conversation, the American is likely to edge away, if he can. Then it may be the turn of the other man to feel uncomfortable. He's been ejected from what was for him a casual zone and stood off in the more formal consultative range.

In this manipulation of space, the communicators are also managing the variety of cues they receive. At very close range, the receiver can pick up markers in several modalities. He can easily be touched. He may be aware of the odors of the other person. He may be aware of his body heat. To the typical American this is an "overload" of information. He would rather stand at a distance where he can see and hear well but not engage other senses. To men in many cultures, however, that is a very deprived communication linkage.

Axis

The human being has a front and a back. This rather obvious fact becomes important in observing how individuals use space. Some arrangements of space encourage people to face each other and to interact. This is called *sociopetal*. Other arrangements encourage individuals to face away from each other. And this often leads to less interaction. This is called *sociofugal*.

This can be seen very easily in the way two people stand in a conversation. Figure 9-1 diagrams the sociopetal-sociofugal dimension in terms of *axis*, the orientation of the body. In the most sociopetal position, the axis of one communicator is parallel to the other and they are face to face. A less sociopetal position is with one participant "giving the shoulder" to the other. In other words, they stand with their shoulders at a 90° angle. Even less interaction is likely if they are standing "shoulder

FIGURE 9-1   Interpersonal Orientation.

The orientation of two communicators can be described in terms of "axis"—
the positioning of bodies. Illustration A represents face-to-face interaction.
B shows a 90° positioning. C demonstrates a shoulder-to-shoulder relationship.
And D illustrates a back-to-back stance. Arrangements that facilitate interaction are called "sociopetal," e.g., A. Arrangements that discourage interaction are called "sociofugal," e.g., D.

to shoulder" both facing the same direction. And the most sociofugal
position is "back to back."

Frequently, communicators will handle close proximity by shifts in
axis. A face-to-face orientation in the "intimate" range will seem like the
prelude to a kiss—an uncomfortable position if one of the participants does
not wish to kiss or be kissed. By turning, the communicators can
maintain proximity but have it feel less intimate. Whispering is easy; but
kissing becomes more difficult.

Position

The fixed arrangement of communicators in space can also foster or
inhibit interaction. Figure 9-2A shows an eight-man conference table. In
such a seating pattern, the man at the "head" of the table usually emerges
as the leader. In addition, there are "hot spots," seats where the participant
tends to talk more. The two ends of the table generate participation. So
do the middle slots on either side. In a regular classroom the students up
the middle of the class tend to participate more, as do the students in
the central front rows. The corner students participate less. A variety of
seating arrangements have been attempted to foster different patterns of
interaction in the classroom. One that is preferred by many is a horseshoe
with the instructor at the end (Figure 9-2B). This arrangement fosters

FIGURE 9-2   Spatial Patterns of Communication.

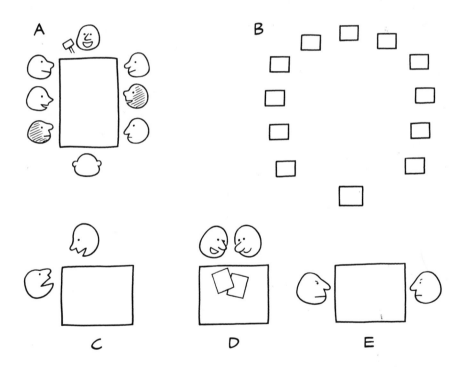

A. At a conference table, some seats lead to greater participation. B. For
class discussion, this is a popular arrangement. C. For conversation, many
prefer a corner of a table. D. Cooperative tasks may be performed side by
side. E. Competitive tasks, meanwhile, draw people to opposite sides of a
table.

interaction among the students but maintains the instructor as a moderator in control.

For different types of interaction, people prefer different seating arrangements. A popular conversational mode is for the pair to sit at the corner of a table (Figure 9-2C). If working on a cooperative task, the side-by-side position is a favorite (Figure 9-2D). In competitive tasks, interactants prefer to sit across the table from each other (Figure 9-2E). Most individuals also have a clear idea how they would monopolize a table, where, for example, they would sit if they wanted to keep a library table to themselves.

Territoriality is a salient feature of animal behavior. Recent studies have revealed elaborate patterns for social control, boundary maintenance, for signaling an intruder. Other studies, such as John Calhoun's work with Norway rats, suggest that overcrowding can cause a startling variety of social pathology.[3] This research, in turn, has raised questions about man's territoriality, his use of space, his crowding in urban centers. Unlike his animal ancestors, man is strongly influenced by learning, by patterns of his culture and his group.[4] But recent work in animal ethology has raised fascinating new questions about the roots of man's common behavior.

MESSAGES OF TIME

For each individual, there is a natural rhythm of time. He eats. He sleeps. His heart beats. His lungs take in air. When he flies long distances east and west, he may suddenly become aware of his inner clock. His tummy will rumble when no one else is hungry. He will be awake when everyone else wants to go to bed. Or he will be drooping while everyone else is still lively. He may on very long journeys suffer disorientation, confusion. Diplomats and businessmen going to important international conferences now try to allow additional time to adjust to the time of the new environment.

In modern, urban, industrial society, man must mesh his activities with the activities of others. He must be punctual—for work, and even for play. He has meetings, and agendas, and timetables. Industrial man is likely to be quite objective about his time. He can "kill time." He can "use time." He can "waste time." In other cultures, time may be less objective. One's life flows on and there may not be a sense that time can be segmented, used, manipulated. Such a thought may seem very inhuman.

[3] John B. Calhoun, "Population Density and Social Pathology," *Scientific American*, 206, Feb. 1962, pp. 139–146.

[4] M. F. A. Montagu, ed., *Man and Aggression* (New York: Oxford University Press, 1968).

Edward Hall has distinguished among the informal, formal, and technical use of time.[5] The informal usage says things take "awhile," or maybe "years." These "years," however, may turn out to be days, months, or centuries. Formal time, in an industrial society, is measured with the calendar or the clock. The businessman says he'll do that "tomorrow," and he does it the next day. He may be disappointed with some associates, particularly in other cultures. When they say "tomorrow" they may be talking "informal" time rather than "formal" time. Technical time is even more precise. It, for example, might distinguish among the solar year, of 365 days, 5 hours, 48 minutes, and 45.51 seconds; the sidereal year, of 365 days, 6 hours, 9 minutes, and 9.54 seconds; and the anamolistic year, of 365 days, 6 hours, 13 minutes, 53.1 seconds.

Communication systems are located in time, and often run for a specified period of time. The formation stage may be set by formal time, informal time, or technical time. Social gatherings may be informal. "Come around eight." And you come well after eight. Business meetings are more formal. "Meet me there at ten." You try to be on time. If you are only a few minutes late you may not mutter apology. But beyond five minutes, you are likely to feel an increasing need for apology. The later you are, the more detailed and lengthy the necessary apology. Communicators in the mass media, where each second may be very valuable, work on technical time. The network TV director cannot start his eight o'clock show five minutes past the hour. The wire service with the story on the wire first—even by seconds—is the wire service that will be used.

The individual's punctuality is likely to reveal his perception of the social occasion, whether he thought it was informal, formal, or technical. Punctuality is also likely to be influenced by the perceived status of the other participants. A man is likely to be more punctual with his boss than with a casual acquaintance. Finally, punctuality is influenced by the individual's own unique personality and experience. Some people are compulsive and anxious about time. Some are oblivious to time. Some are passive-aggressive personalities who use their lateness as a weapon.

To the observer, then, man's punctuality can have sign value. It may reveal things about personality. It may reveal the communicator's attitude toward the other participants in his communication system. It may reveal how he has defined the communication system to himself.

The practicing communicator may, in addition, use time location and time pacing as a purposeful sign. He may wish to emphasize the importance of the communication by placing it "out of phase." An early morning meeting, an evening meeting, a weekend meeting—each is likely to signal something important. Similarly, a late night phone call is likely to signal an urgent message. The communicator who uses such out-of-

[5] Edward T. Hall, *The Silent Language* (Greenwich, Conn.: Fawcett, 1959).

phase emphasis for unimportant messages may, of course, lose credibility very rapidly. It is like the boy who cried "Wolf!"

Finally, the communicator may set careful limits on the total time of the meeting. He puts it in a "time slot." Ideally, he would like to time his communication system so it is fully effective. It should have enough time to effectively solve the problem it faces—but not enough time to wander off on peripheral topics. As Parkinson observes, work expands to fill the available time. The communicator can underscore the importance of an agenda item by having it the only topic to be considered. Or, he can reflect his own value for an item by placing it near the bottom of the agenda where it will be dealt with briefly or even deferred to another time.

In structuring the interpersonal meeting, the communicator may make his visitor time-conscious by asking, when the appointment is made, how much time the caller needs. Once on the scene, the visitor may be given other time cues. He may be seated facing a clock, so he is aware of the passage of time. The communicator may provide performance cues when it is time to leave. And if all else fails, the visitor may be terminated by a secretary or the next appointment.

In this culture, time tends to be used in the business setting *monochronistically*. In other words, time is alloted so that one thing is done at a time. In some cultures, time is not parceled into the same packages. A businessman, for instance, might hold several meetings simultaneously in his office. To the American who is used to having the full attention of other participants, such a use of time may be perceived as very insulting.

SUMMARY

This chapter has explored man's use of time, space, and object, within the communication frame. Objects create slow fading codes. They may be used with communication intent. But their use often serves other non-communicative purposes as well. Therefore, the reader of artifactual codes must infer the degree of intent and awareness that influenced the sign producer; he must sort the symbol from the signal or symptom. The sign value of the artifact may continue after the producer has left. In some cases, they are messages addressed "to whom it may concern." The artifactual codes can be used effectively, however, to structure communication systems, to signal definitions of the situation, to index status, to regulate interaction.

Time and space form the backdrop of all communication systems. But the location of communicators in space, and the time location of the communication system, may have important consequences. Communicators may stand near or far. They may adopt an axis which puts them face to face—or back to back. They may take a stance which is sociopetal, fostering interaction, or a stance which is sociofugal, inhibiting interaction. Similarly, in our use of time, we can signal our definition of a communication system: whether we think it's formal, informal, or technical. We can communicate insult, by being late, or in refusing to use time monochronistically. In short, we can draw time and space out of the background to create signs which facilitate communication—or make it impossible.

DISCUSSION–EXERCISES

1. Think about a common article of clothing such as jeans. List the situations where jeans are appropriate dress. List some situations where jeans would be inappropriate dress. How do your lists compare with the lists of others?

2. Think of an artifact that you use as a symbol. Think of one you use as a signal.

3. Experiment with interpersonal space. Stand "too close" to someone. What happens? Stand "too far" from someone. What happens?

4. Think about the office of the most important person you have ever visited. What did the artifacts and use of space suggest about that person?

5. If you wanted to monopolize a library table (i.e., if you didn't want anyone else to join you), where would you sit? Would you face the door or away from the door?

6. If an invitation were extended for "eight o'clock," what time would you arrive—if it was a party? A dinner? A business appointment?

10

messages of the media

This chapter is designed to

1. Introduce you to the mediatory codes, the signs which are generated in the use of media.

2. Introduce you to the following new terms:
   - time-binding
   - space-binding
   - message time
   - event time
   - message space
   - event space
   - sequential syntax
   - synchronic syntax

3. Introduce you to the concept of *communication band* and to the notion of interband organization, including
   - independence
   - relatedness
     - *redundant*
     - *complementary*
     - *conflicting*

4. Review and expand on such terms as:
   - analogic
   - icon
   - schematic
   - abstraction
   - symbol
   - signal

5. Provide you with an example of mediatory codes in action (e.g., the Nixon–Kennedy televised debate).

THOUGHT STARTERS

1. Can you think of examples of where the media, such as film or television, use performance *signals* as purposeful *symbols*? How about artifactual signals? Spatio-temporal signals?

2. What signs arise in the media that are not available in interpersonal communication?

"Well, maybe we could go to a movie."
"I don't like movies."
"Why not?"
"They're too real."

Marshall McLuhan has argued that: "The medium is the message."[1] McLuhan, in turn, got some of his best ideas from Harold A. Innis, an economic historian. Innis noted that some media are "time-binding," and some are "space-binding."[2] Media such as telephone, telegraph, radio, and television allow man to extend his reach across space. He can instantaneously be in touch with other men, on the far side of the globe, or the far side of the moon. Messages from these media are, however, short-lived. They are not "time-binding." Meanwhile, messages in the print media, in paintings, statues, and monuments, last. They are not as easily transported across space. But they are more permanent.

Innis saw societies leaning toward time-binding or space-binding media. And this orientation, in turn, influences all man's other institutions: family, government, religion. He saw time-binding societies as hierarchical, traditional, sacred. Meanwhile, space-binding societies were seen as segmented, fast-changing, secular. Innis argued that a balance was needed. And he viewed with some alarm the modern trend toward increasingly space-spanning media.

The media mass produce and reproduce messages. Just as the industrial revolution made goods available to a mass market, so modern communication technology makes messages available to a mass audience. The industrial revolution made a profound difference in the way man works

[1] Marshall McLuhan, *Understanding Media* (New York: McGraw-Hill, 1966).
[2] Harold A. Innis, *The Bias of Communication* (Toronto: University of Toronto Press, 1951).

and lives. It changed his total environment, touching most of the material goods he buys and consumes. Similarly, the mass production of messages has made a profound impact on man's intellectual environment. Just as the modern, mass-produced automobile differs from the hand-made sled, so mass-media messages differ from the homespun messages men exchange in private. Media messages can be more complex, slicker, more polished. They surround us in an information affluence unknown to pre-industrial man. This chapter explores the codes that emerge as man moves to media.

THE CODING DIMENSION

The ABX-X' model sketches a "coding dimension" between events (X) and the messages (X') about those events. We noted that a major factor in this dimension is "iconicity," the degree to which the symbol in a message resembles the object being referred to. A life-size, full-color, three-dimensional model is highly iconic. A two-dimensional photograph is less iconic. A drawing may be less iconic still. A name is not iconic at all; it is usually an "arbitrary" assignment.

In face-to-face interaction, some gestures can be iconic. I may re-enact what I did at an earlier time. Or I may act out what I plan to do in the future. Some gestures, such as drawing the finger across the throat, are somewhat iconic; they mimic a knife, they signal "the end." As we move into media, however, we have an expanded capacity to present iconic symbols. We can show movies, photographs, drawings, charts. We can present recordings. We can even reproduce smells, as in 3M's Scratch-N-Sniff.

Just as the individual object may be represented by an iconic symbol, the larger event may be represented analogically in time and space. The media message may reproduce the event moment by moment through time. The message may preserve the space arrangements which were inherent in the event.

In addition, the media message can introduce new markers which do not exist in the real world at all. It can generate signs of its own, peculiar to that medium. These signs, in turn, can comment, illustrate, underscore, elaborate. For example, television's split screen or instant replay provides a view which is not available in the normal world. The media communicator can use stop action, or slow motion. He can add circles or arrows or color cues to highlight key elements.

Finally, the media communicator can manipulate the verbal and the nonverbal bands. He can pull apart their natural relationship and introduce totally new information. He can caption and recaption a photograph. He can present a slide and change the commentary. He can remove the sound track of a movie or videotape and replace it with a totally different set of noises, recorded in a different place and at a different time. He can separate the bands so that they are totally independent. Or he can relate them in a way that is redundant, each band reinforcing the other. He can also supplement, letting each band elaborate on the message. And he can introduce conflict, so that one band contradicts the other.

ANALOGIC IN TIME

For some events, the communicator may wish to preserve the total time and the time sequence of the original event. For others, he would prefer to have "message time," the time it takes to decode the message, considerably shorter than "event time," the length of time covered by the original event (see Figure 10-1). And in still other situations, he would like to slow down the actual event and take a closer look.

An historical motion picture may cover two centuries of events in a couple of hours. Similarly, in a series of time-lapse photographs, the growth of a plant over months may be reproduced in minutes. In the vast majority of media messages, the communicator has dropped out unimportant aspects of the event. He presents an edited version which shows only the highlights. He condenses the event so that the receiver can "save time."

In some instances, however, the communicator wants to preserve the timing of the original event. It may be important to see just how the actual event unfolded in real time. This is frequently used in scientific photography. But it has also been used in entertainment films. For example, pop artist Andy Warhol has produced movies by turning the camera on and letting it run—for hours. Finally, some events go by so rapidly that they cannot be appreciated. The media can slow down such events, stretching time so that the audience can examine what were originally micromomentary happenings. Again, this technique has important applications in scientific communication. It is common in news photos, where we can examine at leisure the moment captured on film.

The communicator can also juggle the time sequence. This is, of course, done constantly in shooting motion pictures. Scenes in the same location or using the same actors are shot at one time. Then later an editor goes back and rearranges the scenes into the proper sequence of the movie. This may be done in documentaries and newsreels. But changing the time sequence can change the message in other ways. It can create the appearance of causal links.

FIGURE 10-1   Event Time and Message Time.

I.

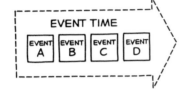

I illustrates an event in real time; the event, in turn, was a sequence of four subevents A, B, C, and D.

II.

MESSAGE TIME:
REDUCTION

II illustrates a message in which the event time has been collapsed, providing a message which takes less time than the original event. II.1 is an example where all the elements have been preserved. II.2 illustrates another way to collapse time: subelements B and C have simply been dropped.

III.

MESSAGE TIME:
SAME

A B C D

III illustrates an example of message time corresponding to event time.

IV.

MESSAGE TIME:
EXPANSION

A B C D

IV illustrates time expansion, where message time is actually longer than event time. An example would be slow-motion photography.

V.

MESSAGE TIME:
RE-ORDERING

D A

V illustrates the reordering of events; D is placed ahead of A, whereas in real time the order was reversed.

A few years ago, the House Un-American Activities Committee produced a film called "Operation Abolition." It purported to show the events during a series of committee hearings in San Francisco. During the hearings, rioting broke out. The committee implied in the film that the riots were communist led and inspired. The American Civil Liberties Union, however, took exception to the film treatment. They produced an answer called "Operation Correction." In it, they pointed out that the committee had shuffled events, showing scenes out of sequence. This made it seem that some events had triggered other events, whereas actually they had been reversed in real time.

ANALOGIC IN SPACE

Typically, messages are not "life-sized." Like event time, event space is usually condensed in a message. But in some cases, it is important to preserve actual size and relationships. And, in some instances, it is necessary to expand, presenting a message which is "larger than life." The motion-picture screen and the outdoor billboard present human figures which are giant-sized. They must be so for all to see (see Figure 10-2).

In the Soviet Union a few years ago, I was struck with the enormous portraits of Lenin scattered throughout the country. At that time there was no advertising, so where an American would expect to see a billboard or a sign on the side of a building, the Soviet citizen was likely to see Lenin's head, with some famous quotation. Lenin's body is, of course, preserved and displayed in his tomb on Red Square. The visitor can go and see the actual man. Usually, when seeing a famous person in the flesh, I think, "There he is, big as life." But upon seeing Lenin, my reaction was, "There he is, *small* as life." He was a little man. And that was startlingly apparent after seeing hundreds of mammoth portraits.

Just as time sequences can be juggled, space relationships can be manipulated. A famous example arose in American politics a few years ago. Senator Joseph McCarthy of Wisconsin was feuding with Senator Millard Tydings of Maryland. In Senator Tydings's bid for reelection, someone from the McCarthy camp introduced a "composite" photo into the campaign. The photo showed Tydings smiling and apparently taking advice from a man who was whispering in his ear. The man was the head of the American Communist Party. The two men, of course, had never appeared in such a pose. The picture was made from two separate photos, taken at different times. They were skillfully blended into one and retouched to look like the record of an actual event. Tydings protested the unethical tactic. But he lost the election. Such tactics, of course, caught up with McCarthy, who was eventually censured by the United States Senate. In part, his downfall was precipitated by the televised Army–Mc-

FIGURE 10-2   Event Space and Message Space.

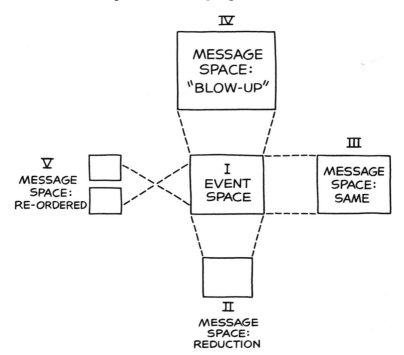

I represents an event in space.

II illustrates message–space reduction; the message takes less space than the actual event.

III illustrates a message space which is "life-sized" (i.e., the event space has been preserved in the message).

IV illustrates a "blow-up," where message space is larger than event space.

V illustrates a message space in which the arrangements of elements in space have been reordered. In the rearranging, event space may be reduced, preserved, or expanded.

Carthy hearings, during which the public got its first close look at the senator via a nonverbal media.

ICONICITY OF OBJECT

Any physical object has shape, outline, size, texture, color, and dimensionality in space. It may also have inner structure. It may have functions and workings. As we noted earlier, the analogic symbol may be (a) an icon, (b) a schematic, or (c) an abstraction. The first reproduces the outward appearance of the object (e.g., its shape, color, texture). The schematic usually "takes the skin off" the object. It gives a peek at the inner structure and workings. Blueprints and maps are schematics. Finally, the abstraction may draw on both appearance and workings, presenting a sign which captures the "feel" or "spirit" or "function" of the object. Many modern paintings, such as "Nude Descending A Staircase," are symbols of this order. For the icon, denotative meaning is usually clear. For the schematic, we frequently need a verbal key, or a set of well-learned analogic symbols (Figure 10-3). The denotative meaning may be less clear than with the icon. Finally, with the abstraction, denotative meaning may be quite ambiguous. Nevertheless, the abstraction may elicit strong connotative meanings.

For the communicator, these different signs may have different advantages. The communicator who wants his audience to be able to identify an object will use the icon. On the other hand, if the audience must be able to deal with the object's inner workings, its construction and

FIGURE 10-3   Analogic Symbols.

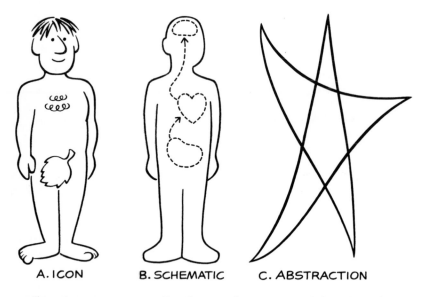

A. ICON   B. SCHEMATIC   C. ABSTRACTION

Illustration *a* represents an "icon"; outward appearance of the referent has been preserved. Illustration *b* represents a "schematic"; it shows the inner structure. Other examples would be a map or a blueprint. Illustration *c* is an "abstraction." It looks like the figure of a man, but it also resembles a star. It may elicit strong connotative feelings even though its denotative meaning is ambiguous.

function, then a schematic may be best. And finally, the abstraction may be important in eliciting necessary feelings from the audience. It may teach the affective side of the object.

OTHER SYMBOLS AND SIGNALS

The media communicator has the additional option of inventing signs which have never been seen before. Some of these, in turn, become part of the visual or sound vocabulary available to other media communicators. Many trademarks and logos are in this category. So are political symbols, such as the G.O.P. elephant or the Democratic donkey. Another example would be the "red cross," which was used traditionally to mark (or index) military hospitals and ambulances. It then became the logo of the International Red Cross. Variations of this symbol led to other commercial trademarks, such as Blue Cross. In non-Christian countries, relief agencies often use the red symbolism, but do not use the cross. In Moslem countries, for example, the League of Red Cross Societies is represented by the Red Crescent. In Iran, the Red Lion and Sun is used. And in Israel, the relief organization uses a red Star of David.

The media can also introduce signals which act as pointers or indexers. The comic strip, as a simple example, has a whole repertoire of signs which tell the reader whether the character is thinking or talking, sleeping or swearing, moving or standing still. Similarly, other media, such as television, film, and recordings, have their signal sets for special messages. Classically, for example, a "dissolve" in cinema meant a major shift of scene or time. The "cut," a simple change of view, was used within a scene, for example, in "cutting" from one actor to another. Television, however, has introduced the "cut" even when there has been a major move in time or space. This, in turn, is becoming an increasingly frequent technique in cinema. Through a variety of created signs, the media communicator can signal coming events, point to important objects, and index events in terms of the larger message.

BANDS: VERBAL AND NONVERBAL

In each media system the communicators are linked by at least one communication "band" and usually by two: the verbal and the nonverbal. The communicator receives markers, intimately, through his sense modalities. In turn, the markers are brought to his sensory receptors by a variety of communication channels: telephone lines, newspapers, radio and television, tape recordings, and so on. The concept of a *communication band* cuts across channels and modalities to sort verbal and nonverbal markers within a communication system. In media, the communicator has a unique opportunity to select, organize, and manipulate bands.

A single marker may involve more than one sense modality. A simple handshake, for example, presents a visual marker of the two hands meeting. It presents a pressure marker on the hand. And it presents a thermal marker, whether the other chap is hot and sweaty or cold and clammy. The closeness of the other individual may, in fact, engage olfaction. On the verbal side, the perception of speech may involve more than one sense, especially in some circumstances. We listen. But, particularly if we are having trouble hearing, or perhaps can't understand the accent of the speaker, we also watch his lips and pick up additional cues. We use eyes plus ears.

Media systems differ in the bands they make available: verbal, nonverbal, or both. They also differ in the "band width" or "band capacity" of each available band. When communicators are linked by a telephone call, they have a narrow, and primarily verbal, band capacity. It makes little difference what each is wearing, whether they smile or frown, glance at their watch, or gaze out the window. There is no nonverbal band to make these cues available. Similarly, with two businessmen corresponding, a narrow, verbal band is employed.

On the other hand, the television producer has a much expanded band width. He can send both verbal and nonverbal messages. And in each band he has more options. He can, for example, send a greater variety of sound markers, with higher fidelity, than he could over the telephone. Similarly, he can present an enormous range of visual markers, at the same time and in quick succession. The television producer, however, does not have the same band capacity available in face-to-face interaction. He cannot touch. He cannot smell. He cannot taste. He isn't able to present some of the markers of full, three-dimensional color. On the other hand, the television communicator has an array of symbols in his repertoire that the face-to-face speaker does not have. He has the mediatory codes we've already discussed: cutting, dissolving, changing camera angle, reversing image, split screens, and so on. In addition, he can match up the verbal and nonverbal bands in unique ways. He can pair a verbal band produced at one time with a nonverbal band produced in a different time and place.

Comparing the verbal and nonverbal bands, the latter appears to have greater band capacity. The verbal band depends on two sense modalities; the nonverbal can use all five senses, although it may not use all five at once. In the verbal band, the encoder uses either his voice to produce sound markers, or he uses his hand to produce writing. The verbal decoder uses either his ears to hear the sound markers or his eyes to read the print markers. Meanwhile, the nonverbal band can handle markers in any mode: sight, sound, touch, taste, smell.

One-Way, Two-Way

In the face-to-face communication situation, the verbal band tends to be one-directional, one-user-at-a-time, and alternating. In other words, speakers take turns using the verbal band. It's impolite to talk while someone else has the floor. Speaker switching is regulated very formally in large parliamentary meetings. It is also regulated by an elaborate set of signals in the small interpersonal group. Meanwhile, both communicators can be using the nonverbal band at the same time. It is two-way and simultaneous. The speaker, while talking, can also gesture for emphasis. Meanwhile, at the same instant, the hearer can be frowning, or smiling, or falling asleep. He can provide, nonverbally, simultaneous feedback to the speaker's verbal and nonverbal messages.

For a long time, media systems tended to be one-way, whether they employed the verbal band, as in radio and newspapers, or both bands, as in television. Increasingly, however, media technology is providing two-way communication. Radio talk shows encourage phone calls, which in turn are put out over the air. And "broad band" television nets allow the communicator to send as well as receive.

Interband Relationships

Information in the two bands can be (a) independent, or (b) related. If the latter, they can be (a) redundant, (b) complementary, or (c) conflicting. Even within each band, signs may have these relationships. The phrase "That's nice" may be said with a reinforcing intonation pattern which makes it a compliment. Or, it can be said with a conflicting intonation which changes the meaning from pleasantness to bitter irony. A communicator may present two nonverbal gestures at the same time, for example a smile and a hand gesture. They may be totally independent. Or they may be related, to provide the same information again (e.g., the smile plus the A-Okay sign). They may be related, to provide supplemental information (e.g., the smile, plus pointing at the object which is causing happiness). Or they could be related to provide conflicting or countermanding information (e.g., the smile plus an obscene gesture). When the communicator has both verbal and nonverbal bands available, he can do the same thing among bands. He has an expanded range of relationships available among markers; he can produce increasingly complex organizations in his message system.

In interpersonal communication, the verbal and the nonverbal bands tend to be redundant, but they can be independent or even conflicting. The speaker may scratch while he talks, not as an illustrator or as a regulator, but simply because he happens to itch at that moment. He'd itch no matter what he was saying. Frequently, however, the speaker's verbal and nonverbal bands are closely meshed, as in the use of illustrators. When they appear to conflict, this may be taken as purposeful. The communicator is meaning to be ironic or satirical. Or it may be taken as a clue to deception, or as a symptom of a disturbed emotional state.

The psychiatrist, of course, is very sensitive to inconsistencies in the verbal and nonverbal band. If, for example, the client says he loves his wife, but takes off his wedding ring every time he mentions her, this may be taken by the psychiatrist as a sign of inner conflict. The man is verbalizing one thing, but his actions betray other feelings. Similarly, we may be able to ferret out "false notes" in the performance of another. We may be particularly on guard when dealing with a salesman, a job interviewer, or a politician, or someone who might be motivated to put on a "false front."

When we do detect a false note, we are likely to believe the cues we have picked up in the nonverbal band. We often feel that these cues are harder to control. They are more likely to be out of awareness. They, therefore, may be more reliable indicators than the words which the speaker spins out.

Particularly in the media, the conflict between bands can be used creatively to structure new meanings. In the movies, the "montage" places seemingly unrelated scenes together, creating a new whole, with a different meaning than any of the elements. A shot of a burning house might be paired with a child crying in the street. This, in turn, might be joined by a picture of an airplane flying through the air. Suddenly, the sequence begins to suggest "war"—instead of a kid who wants candy, an arson at work, or an airliner on a pleasure cruise. Similarly, the media communicator can present telling cues in one band to provide counterpoint for the other band. A well-placed wink, or a hand gesture, or a close-up from a particular angle may place what is being said in the verbal band in a whole new context. It may force reinterpretation on a different plane.

Sequential or Synchronic

A potentially important difference between the verbal and nonverbal bands is this: the verbal band uses *sequential syntax* through time while the nonverbal band may use both *sequential* and *synchronic syntax*. In other words, the "sign patterns" provided by the bands differ. The verbal band is one-dimensional. The nonverbal band is multidimensional. Written or spoken language is linear. It is encoded and transmitted word by word over time. The decoding process may actually be very complex. It may involve a series of expectations. It may require storage and reinterpretation in terms of succeeding events. But reception, too, is done over time. Meanwhile, an analogic message, such as a motion picture, may have an order through time. But it also has an organization within each frame. There are patterns among the simultaneously presented symbols. A movie director, for example, might want to communicate the message: the villain is now more powerful than the hero. He might do this sequentially, showing first the villain, shot from a low angle, so he appears to be looking down at you. Then he might show the hero, shot from a high angle, so he appears to be looking up. Or the director might communicate his message synchronically, at the same time, in one shot, by showing a side view of the villain towering over the hero. In the film, the director, of course, has other nonverbal symbols he could simultaneously manipulate toward the same message: facial expression, body posture, artifacts, and so on. This all adds up to a powerful armory of signs available to the media communicator.

While examples of media use—and abuse—abound, some of the most interesting grow out of the political sphere. The introduction of powerful nonverbal media, such as television, has raised new concerns about the subtle and pervasive influences of nonverbal messages.

NIXON AND KENNEDY DEBATE

Television first became a factor in the national political scene in the election of 1948, between Harry S Truman and Thomas E. Dewey. At that time, only the northeastern section of the country had television. But the Democratic convention was held in Philadelphia, and for the first time, voters got a close look at a significant part of the political process.

One event at that convention is attributed by some to be the factor which helped Truman upset the expected winner. The Democrats adopted a strong civil rights platform, and Truman stuck his neck out to endorse that stand. It meant, in turn, a walk-out of Southern delegates. The television cameras picked up the scene of the Southerners walking by a table and depositing their delegate badges. Some have speculated that this dramatic scene may have had a powerful impact on liberals and blacks who were watching. It may have mobilized them to Truman's support. Interestingly, the scene was apparently staged by a television cameraman who wanted a way to dramatize the conflict. While the Southerners did split with Truman, they kept their badges and their convention privileges.

The 1960 Campaign

The major emergence of television in politics came, however, over a decade later, in the 1960 contest between John F. Kennedy and Richard M. Nixon. Kennedy made effective use of television, even in his bid for the nomination. He defeated Hubert Humphrey in the crucial West Virginia primary, in large part through a well-financed television campaign. Humphrey, at that time untutored in the use of television, spent most of his television budget on one half-hour show just before election. Running an open telephone line, he promised to answer all callers. But unscreened, the callers turned out to be mostly the opposition, people who would ask embarrassing questions rather than let Humphrey present his more popular views, nuts who would harangue the candidate endlessly without letting him respond, individuals who would ask pointless, involved, low-interest questions, chewing up the candidate's precious time. In short, Humphrey spent his meager resources treating the opposition to an exposure of their best points, not his.

When Kennedy won the nomination, the Republican and Democratic contestants agreed to debate on television, an historic first. In retrospect, this agreement itself was probably an advantage for Kennedy. At the time, he was still the relatively unknown junior senator from Massachusetts. Meanwhile, Richard Nixon had served as vice president for eight years with great public exposure under a very popular president.

Going into the first television debate, the polls showed Nixon ahead in the race. But after that debate, Kennedy had inched ahead. And he remained ahead to win the election by a narrow margin. Nearly seventy million Americans watched the first debate, the largest TV audience assembled up to that time. Both candidates were later to credit the TV debate with turning the tide of the election.

Nonverbal Messages

The event was the best studied communication event up to that point in history.[3] Unfortunately, most of the research designs did not look explicitly at one of the factors, which turned out to be most interesting: the impact of nonverbal cues. Anecdotal evidence suggests that those who heard the debate on radio thought it was a draw, perhaps with Nixon having a slight edge. Those who later read the full text of the debate tended to have a similar impression. But among those who *saw* the debate on television, most felt Kennedy came away the victor.

[3] Sidney Kraus (ed.), *The Great Debates* (Bloomington, Ind.: Indiana University Press, 1962).

One study examined what viewers expected of the candidates and then what they thought after the debate.[4] In ratings of performance, the two men did not change on being articulate, concise, and fair, dimensions that are likely to be judged from verbal cues. But on other dimensions, there were striking differences. Kennedy was seen as more interesting than had been expected, more sharp, active, strong, colorful, handsome, relaxed, calm, deep, experienced, wise and virile. Meanwhile, Nixon was moving in the opposite direction. He was seen as more boring than had been expected, more dull, passive, old, weak, colorless, ugly, tense, agitated, shallow, inexperienced, foolish, and sterile. While both men were trying to make their very best appearance, one was producing markers that were interpreted as very positive signs, while the other was not (see Figure 10-4).

Performance Cues

Much has been made of Mr. Nixon's makeup on the night of the first debate. But that was merely one of many problems that plagued his performance.[5] He had, first of all, been ill. He had lost weight. And in trying to catch up on his schedule, he had put in a full day of campaigning before hostile labor crowds in Chicago. Senator Kennedy, meanwhile, had spent the day at his hotel, resting and reviewing with his advisors his strategy for the debate. He had just finished campaigning in California and he looked fit and tan.

In posture, Kennedy stood erect. He illustrated with his right hand, making sharp batons to punctuate his points. Meanwhile, Nixon was suffering with an injured knee. He stood on one leg, gripping the podium with both hands. He perspired freely. And he looked tense.

In facial features, Nixon has medially downturned eyebrows and a mouth that pulls down at the corners. It is a "frozen affect" display associated with anger. Kennedy had brows that raised slightly in the center. They tended to give him a concerned, sympathetic appearance.

Artifactual Cues

Nixon was not wearing television makeup as such. He does have very light skin, and very dark hair. As a result he can appear unshaven even when he has just had a shave. That evening he was freshly shaved. And

---

[4] Percy H. Tannenbaum, Bradley S. Greenberg, and F. R. Silverman, "Candidate Images," in Sidney Kraus (ed.), *The Great Debates* (Bloomington, Ind.: Indiana University Press, 1962), p. 283.

[5] Theodore H. White, *The Making of the President 1960* (New York: Atheneum, 1961), pp. 340–354.

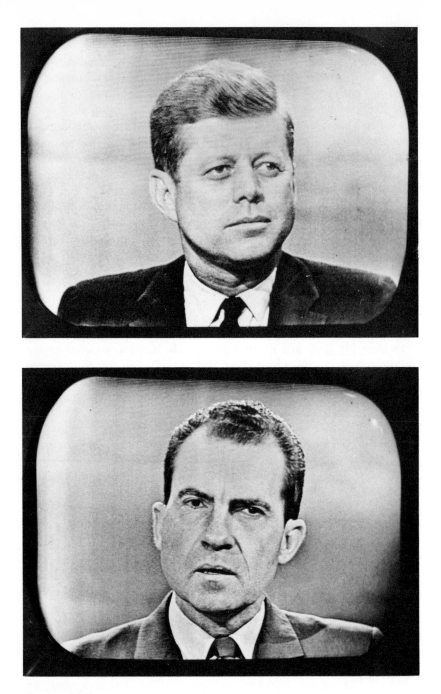

FIGURE 10-4

Senator John F. Kennedy and then Vice President Richard M. Nixon, as they appeared during their first television debate, September 26, 1960.

he used an after-shave powder stick on his beard. Unfortunately, as he perspired during the evening, the powder streaked, making it appear that he was wearing makeup, and making his beard all the more evident. Nixon wore a light suit and a light tie. Kennedy wore a dark tie and suit, that contrasted more sharply with the background. While listening to Nixon, Kennedy was busy scribbling with his pencil, shaking his head and appearing to disagree. Nixon, meanwhile, sat gripping his knee, nodding in apparent agreement with what Kennedy was saying. Nixon had requested that the television director not show shots of him while he was wiping his face with a handkerchief. For the most part, this request was followed, although he was caught in one long-shot. Nixon's loss of weight made his clothing appear to fit badly. The neck of his coat collar gapped. And his stance caused wrinkles to appear across the front of his jacket.

Mediatory Cues

The networks had made every attempt to assure equal treatment for the two candidates. But several things occurred that underscore the availability of mediatory cues. The backdrop was supposed to be darker. But the paint kept drying light. It was still wet from the last painting attempt when the show went on the air. New tubes had been put in all the cameras to ensure the best possible reception. This, in turn, only accentuated the problem with Nixon's beard. Small "inky" spotlights had been placed to shine into Nixon's eyes, helping to alleviate the dark shadows under his heavy brows. But just before air time, still photographers had been let on the set to take some shots. And in the milling around, these small floor "inkies" were jarred out of place. The director tried to give equal exposure to the two candidates, but a count reveals that more reaction shots were taken of Kennedy than of Nixon. It was, however, the Kennedy lieutenants who complained. They are reported to have said, "Keep the camera on Nixon. Every time his face appears on the screen, he loses votes."

In summary, the television watcher probably saw many minute markers that for him had sign value. He was examining his next president. One of these two men was going to serve as chief executive at a very critical point in history. And the viewing voter made a series of inferences from the nonverbal cues he saw.

SUMMARY

This chapter examined codes of the media, the markers that can arise in the employment of print, pictures, models, charts. Moving to media, the communicator has additional options, in the iconicity of his symbols, in the analogies of time and space, in the introduction of media-specific markers that can reinforce, complement, or contradict. He has the opportunity to combine communication bands in ways that are not possible in "real life."

The example of the Nixon–Kennedy debate underscores the subtle cues that are available. The media communicator can take advantage of the performance, artifactual, and spatio-temporal codes. And he can embellish them with mediatory codes, markers unique to his chosen medium.

DISCUSSION–EXERCISES

1. Watch a television drama with the sound turned off. Without the verbal band, what nonverbal signs do you become aware of?

2. See a foreign film in a language you do not know. (Pick one, if possible, with neither subtitles nor English dubbing of sound; most likely, however, you will have to settle for one with English subtitles.) Watch the film, listening to the sound, including the voice patterns—but try not to read the subtitles. What nonverbal signs do you notice?

3. Study a well-illustrated magazine. What signs emerge in this medium that are not available in interpersonal communication?

4. Take a simple symbol such as the cross. Where do you find it appearing besides the Red Cross and Blue Cross? Analyze another simple sign, such as the five-point star.

5. Think about a situation, such as a speech or presentation, where you could introduce mediatory codes that you would not normally use. What code elements can you use? Would this be more effective? Take more effort for you? Less effort for your audience?

Film Tips

Some of the examples mentioned in this chapter are available in many university film libraries, in particular: (a) the House Un-American Activities Committee film, "Operation Abolition," and the American Civil Liberties Union film, "Operation Correction," and (b) the first Nixon–Kennedy television debate.

Each of these films is long, and a sample may provide enough material for a good class discussion. "Operation Abolition" and "Operation Correction" are quite redundant and can be boring if both are seen in the same viewing session. It is effective to look at "Operation Abolition" in one class session and discuss the possible impact on its original target audience and then to look at "Operation Correction" during the next class period and discuss its impact; in particular, did it in turn manipulate mediatory codes? If only one film is used, "Operation Abolition" is more pertinent to the discussion of mediatory codes.

With the Nixon–Kennedy debate, an effective technique is to view the first six to nine minutes with the sound turned off. Viewers typically feel they've "seen everything" in a few moments of this; but then they begin to be aware of more and more nonverbal cues. After discussing this silent presentation, if time permits, it is interesting to watch the rest of the debate with the sound turned on and discuss the difference.

Two other films are interesting in relation to the content of this chapter. "Point of Order" is a Canadian film about the 1954 Army–McCarthy hearings. As we have noted, the nonverbal cues given off by Senator Joseph McCarthy made many people change their opinion of him. A second film of interest is "Triumph of the Will," a Nazi propaganda film of the 1930s. It is an interesting example of an early and, at the time, very powerful use of nonverbal media.

11

-plications:
im-, ap-, and com-

LEARNING TIPS

This chapter is designed to

1. Summarize the importance of nonverbal communication in terms of (a) amount, (b) impact, (c) awareness, and (d) increase.

2. Underscore the assumptions of *effectiveness* and *efficiency* in our use of nonverbal communication.

3. Review key facets of nonverbal communication, in terms of (a) communicator roles, and (b) sign processes.

4. Point to implications for us as nonverbal communicators.

5. Provide you with whiter teeth and a happier sex life. (I just wanted to see if you were still awake.)

THOUGHT STARTERS

1. How will you apply your new knowledge of nonverbal communication?

"Would you like to go out with me again?"
"No."
"Oh."

OUR JOURNEY INTO THE NONVERBAL DOMAIN is nearing an end. We started on a simple plain, looking at two cartoon gentlemen standing beside a rocket. We then took a quick fantasy flight ourselves, to the Land of +. From that overview we began to see some of the challenges ahead of us in the nonverbal domain. Returning, some crude maps in hand, we started the difficult task of exploring in earnest. We began hacking our way through some difficult intellectual terrain, meeting and conquering new terms, new perspectives. Intermittently in our travels we caught glimpse of some familiar figures: Al and Bill and Xan. Now we have reached the end of a long, difficult climb. It is time to look back on what we have accomplished. It is time to reflect on the meaning of what we have done. And it is time to look ahead, to other challenges that still remain in the nonverbal world.

REVIEW

We might begin our review by making explicit some assumptions which have guided our exploration in the nonverbal realm. First, we have assumed that by knowing about nonverbal cues, by understanding the process of nonverbal communication, we can be more *effective* in our relations with other people. Stated abstractly, we would like to be more effective in forming, operating, and terminating communication systems. In more human terms, we hope that our new knowledge about nonverbal communication would help us: establish more meaningful relationships; encourage and maintain relationships that are healthy, stimulating, and significant; contribute productively to relationships that are creative and rewarding; successfully conclude relationships that are exhausted and barren; change and manage the communication situations of our daily life, generating and regenerating, fostering nourishment and growth.

Second, knowledge about nonverbal communication may make us more *efficient* as well as more effective. We may be able to achieve the same effect with less effort, less time, less worry, fewer heartaches. We may be able to conserve valuable resources: manpower, money, materials. All of us have hopes and aspirations, for ourselves, our family and friends, our community and society. But each of us has a limited time on this earth. And we do not have an inexhaustible supply of talent, energy, wealth. We need to be wise in our use of precious life.

In this book we have looked at man the communicator. We have looked at his communication systems. We have examined his codes. We have explored, in particular, the many nonverbal signs which man uses to touch the mind and heart of his fellow man. From our explorations, a number of conclusions emerge:

- *First, an enormous amount of nonverbal communication goes on around us.* The naive communicator may think of communication primarily in terms of the spoken or written word. But once we begin to take a closer look at human communication we become increasingly aware of the vast array of nonverbal signs available to man. We realize that almost every communication situation has a nonverbal component—and frequently a very large component.
- *Second, the nonverbal component can have an important impact.* It can produce important consequences in the communication situation. It can influence the outcome of communication systems. It may shape the decisions made by the individual, the group, the larger society. We find the nonverbal component at work in our selection of products, partners, programs, and presidents.
- *Third, nonverbal communication often operates at low levels of awareness.* Frequently, communicators do not appear to realize that they are sending—or receiving—nonverbal cues. This, of course, makes us particularly vulnerable to the sophisticated manipulator who does know what he is doing. It also means that it is difficult to analyze communication breakdowns; it's hard to spot just what went wrong when misunderstandings do arise.
- *Fourth, nonverbal communication appears to be growing in importance.* Modern technology increasingly facilitates the transmission of nonverbal signs; examples include television, cinema, computer-aided graphic displays,

holographs, high-fidelity recordings, communication satellites, and high-speed color printing processes. Similarly, our environment is increasingly man-made—from giant skyscrapers to sprawling freeways to common household trinkets. The landscape is dotted with "to whom it may concern" messages. Modern man surrounds himself with artifacts which appeal, direct, beckon, command. In the modern urban environment we also interact with an increasing number of strangers. Unlike the classic folk society, our environment is not populated with friends and relatives who knew us from birth. Frequently in interacting with these strangers we use nonverbal cues to guide our responses. We count on nonverbal signs to fill in the past we do not know, to help us discern motives and intentions, to alert us to danger or deception, to open our experience to relationships which extend and expand.

In our exploration of nonverbal communication, we have taken a fresh look at man in his communicator roles, as decoder, processor, encoder, administrator. We have also scrutinized the sign processes man uses to reduce uncertainty about his social environment. Let us recap the key concepts in these two areas.

Communicator Roles

Figure 11-1 summarizes our perspective on man, the communicator. We have suggested that man moves through his world, increasing and decreasing uncertainty, through direct experience, but equally importantly, through communication. Man, the information organism, feeds on the symbolic markers in his environment. Some of these markers (1) may be "missed cues," stimuli which, for him, have no symbolic meaning. On others, he may "miscue," placing a misinterpretation on the stimulus he sees. But many of these markers are decoded (2) and provide the basis of his response to the world he knows. Markers with sign values are processed (3), and this in turn may lead the communicator to encode (4) new markers, which become potential signs for other communicators.

In addition to his roles as decoder, processor, and encoder, modern man increasingly plays the role of systems administrator (5). He arranges systems in which he is a participant. And he constructs and launches and supervises communication systems where other communicators encode, process, and decode. These communication systems may differ in (a) structure, (b) function, and (c) evolution. They may have few elements and simple interrelationships. Or, they may have many elements, in a complex superstructure. Their activities may be directed toward the environment, toward functions of the system, or toward the needs of the members. They may have long, uninterrupted histories, intermittent cycles of

FIGURE 11-1   Communicator Roles.

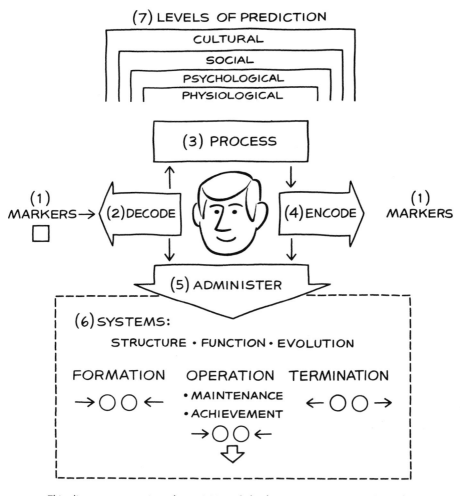

This diagram summarizes the activities of the human communicator. (See the text.)

activity, or brief encounters. Frequently, however, we can note distinct phases: formation, when the system comes into being; operation, when the system maintains itself and moves toward goals; and termination, when the system deactivates.

Finally, we have suggested that in explaining and predicting (7) man's communication behavior, we may need to look at the cultural, social, psychological, and physiological levels. Some communication patterns are learned by all who grow up in a specific culture. Some communication behaviors are distinct for a group or a particular role in society. And some are unique to the individual, growing out of his personality and experience. Undergirding all of these is the physiological level, which helps us understand what markers man can perceive, what it will be easiest for him to use, how he can move from a stimulus to a complex set of inferences.

Sign Processes

Figure 11-2 illustrates the process we have examined as an event becomes a meaningful sign for some communicator. First, (1) our world is populated with persons, objects, events (and concepts), in time and space (and in imagination). Some of the persons are fellow communicators, sharing an information system with us. They produce codes (2), which may be described as (a) performance, arising out of the body; (b) artifactual, arising in the use of objects; (c) spatio-temporal, emerging in the use of time and space; and (d) mediatory, generated in the use of film, art, music, and so on. In the area of performance codes, we have distinguished other categories: emblems, illustrators, regulators, affect displays, and adaptors. Among illustrators, there are pointers, ideographs, kinetographs, batons, spatials, and pictographs. Regulators include points, positions, and presentations. And adaptors may relate to self, object, or alter (i.e., another person). These codes are transmitted to us through communication bands (3), either verbal or nonverbal. These bands may be independent. Or they may be related: redundant, complementary, or conflicting.

The stimulus itself, as it impinges on our senses, is a marker (3), a sign vehicle. These markers may be enduring, temporary, or momentary. If the marker means something other than itself, we call it a sign (4) for that receiver. Two basic types of sign were distinguished: signals and symbols. In addition, the relationship between the sign and its referent may be analogic and iconic, where the sign in some way resembles the object or event; or it may be digital and artitrary, having a learned rather than a natural association. Among the analogic signs, we further discriminated the icon, the schematic, and the abstraction. Finally, we suggested that signs may elicit meanings (5) from the communicator. A sign may have clear denotative meaning, pointing to a referent. It may also have connotative meanings, a set of associations and elicited feelings. Finally, some signs perform a structural function; they link other signs, and introduce meanings for the larger sign patterns.

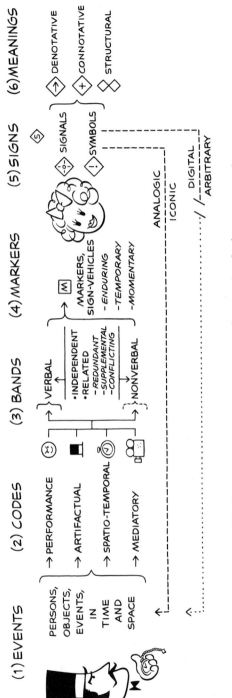

FIGURE 11-2 Sign Processes.

This diagram reviews the process as events become signs for human communicators.
(See the text.)

(1) EVENTS   (2) CODES   (3) BANDS   (4) MARKERS   (5) SIGNS   (6) MEANINGS

PERSONS,
OBJECTS,
EVENTS,
IN
TIME
AND
SPACE

→ PERFORMANCE
→ ARTIFACTUAL
→ SPATIO-TEMPORAL
→ MEDIATORY

VERBAL
•INDEPENDENT
•RELATED
  - REDUNDANT
  - SUPPLEMENTAL
  - CONFLICTING
NONVERBAL

MARKERS,
SIGN-VEHICLES
- ENDURING
- TEMPORARY
- MOMENTARY

SIGNALS
SYMBOLS

DENOTATIVE
CONNOTATIVE
STRUCTURAL

ANALOGIC
ICONIC
DIGITAL
ARBITRARY

187

IMPLICATIONS

What implications might we draw from our search? Perhaps a primary implication is simply this: most of us have a much larger reservoir of nonverbal signs available to us than we usually realize.

Many potentially significant signs are "missed cues." An interesting example is in the area of deception, which was mentioned briefly in the text. Paul Ekman and Wally Friesen have recently distinguished between cues of *deception* and cues of *leakage*. The first are those signals that indicate that deception is taking place; the observer does not know *what* is being held back or covered, but he can detect that something is amiss. In their experiments, Ekman and Friesen have found, for example, that illustrators tend to drop off during deception.[1] This change in the rate of illustrating might be a clue to deception for the astute observer. Similarly, there are indications that a particular type of self-adaptor—touching the face—increases when an individual is lying.

Meanwhile, cues of leakage are those markers that reveal the *nature* of the deception. Nonverbally, the deceiver "spills the beans." An example of this would be a micromomentary facial expression that the communicator tried to conceal but couldn't. The facial expression might reveal how the individual really felt, although he was saying, and trying to portray, something else. Again, the astute observer may be able to detect these cues. He may be able to spot deception, and even more, uncover that which is being concealed.

Even where deception is not involved, we frequently use nonverbal cues to decide whom to interact with: who would be most fun to date, who would be the most credible source for information, who would be most trustworthy as an associate, who would be loyal, brave, kind, courteous, thrifty. . . . We usually find it convenient to use "stereotypes." On the basis of a few gross cues, we are likely to categorize people. We type them, in relation to others we have met or perhaps seen in the mass media. In a study a few years ago, for example, adults responded to youngsters with long hair as "radical," "drug-using," and "promiscuous." The individuals so classified actually had a wide range of political and other beliefs.

Stereotyping is a very efficient reducer of uncertainty; on the basis of a few salient cues we can quickly decide yes or no. But stereotypes are not always effective. It is easy to "miscue," to place an inappropriate interpretation on a salient sign. As we begin to observe more nonverbal

[1] Paul Ekman and Wallace V. Friesen, "Hand Movements," *Journal of Communication*, 22, 1972, pp. 353–374.

signs, and as we gain experience in interpreting nonverbal signs, our predictions about other people are likely to get better. Our two-dimensional, black-and-white stereotypes evolve into more complex—and more useful—inference systems.

As encoders, too, we typically have more nonverbal signs available than we realize. Most of us could probably be more effective communicators if we were able to do three things:

1. *Increase "band width."* In other words, use the nonverbal as well as the verbal band. And use the full possibilities within the nonverbal band. Frequently, we settle for a narrow, verbal band, when we could give our messages more power and impact. We deliver a speech or a report or a lecture in a dry monotone. We don't make full use of available performance codes. Or we don't use mediatory codes: illustrations and audiovisual techniques, films and records, blackboards, and flipcharts. Similarly, in written communication, we may settle for gray text, when we could add a nonverbal dimension, with color, photos, graphs, diagrams.

2. *Make a better selection of nonverbal signs.* As encoders, we have certain goals.[2] We would like to have our receivers select and attend to our messages. We would like to have them comprehend what we are trying to get across. We would like them to accept; to respond with appropriate feelings and emotions. We would like them to be able to recall the information we transmit. And we would like them to be able to use and apply that information in appropriate situations. For each of these goals, we may be able to select nonverbal signs which increase the probability of success. We may, for example, use novel nonverbal signs to attract attention. We may use analogic rather than digital codes to increase understanding. We may use connotative symbols as well as denotative symbols.

3. *Attend to the communication system.* Frequently, we think primarily of the content we are trying to encode, the X-to-X' dimension. We do not consider the A-to-B messages we are encoding, or could encode. With thought, it is possible to facilitate a communication system in forming, operating, achieving. We may need to give prior thought to the spatio-temporal dimension. We may need to consider appropriate time and place. We may want to consider seating arrangement, who will talk to whom, whether to establish an informal environment or a more formal context, whether to foster feedback or encourage a one-way flow.

These suggestions are, of course, mere thought starters. Each of us has unique communication opportunities—and challenges. We play diverse professional roles. We bear different responsibilities as family members and as friends. We shoulder other challenges as citizens, in our

---

[2] Randall Harrison, "Nonverbal Communication: Explorations into Time, Space, Action and Object," in James H. Campbell and Hal W. Hepler (eds.), *Dimensions in Communication* (Belmont, Calif.: Wadsworth, 1972, 2nd ed.).

localities, in our nation, in the international community of man. In all these arenas, however, we have the opportunity to increase the quality of our communication.

CONCLUSION

We have arrived, then, not at the pinnacle of the nonverbal domain, but rather at the first plateau. There are peaks ahead to conquer, certainly in the application of what we have already learned; but also in the new knowledge being discovered, the new research frontiers which are opening constantly.

This first excursion has provided a few crude maps, a few key terms, which may unlock other resources, a few provisions that may nourish your interest for a further quest. Perhaps in some far corner of the nonverbal domain we will meet again.

> "Aren't you even going to kiss me good night?"
> "Stop talking."
> x   x   x   +

DISCUSSION–EXERCISES

1. Consider the implications of what you have learned in this book. List as many as you can. Then select the most promising—and experiment!

12

epilog

Following the tradition launched by Jurgen Ruesch and Weldon Kees and recently revived by Mark Knapp, I would like to conclude this text with a nonverbal message. The photograph is by the talented California artist, Joanne Leonard.

selected, annotated bibliography of further readings

ARGYLE, MICHAEL. *Social Interaction*. New York: Atherton, 1969. Excellent summary and integration of research literature.

BAKER, STEPHEN. *Visual Persuasion*. New York: McGraw-Hill, 1961. An advertising pro looks at visual communication.

BALL, JOHN, and FRANCES C. BYRNES. *Research, Principles, and Practices in Visual Communication*. Washington, D.C.: Department of Audiovisual Instruction, National Education Association, 1964. Becoming dated but still a good sourcebook of relevant communication theory and research.

BARKER, LARRY L., and NANCY B. COLLINS. "Nonverbal and Kinesic Research." In *Methods of Research in Communication*, edited by P. EMMERT and W. W. BROOKS. Boston: Houghton, Mifflin, 1970. An introduction to some of the research problems.

BIRDWHISTELL, RAY L. *Kinesics and Context*. Philadelphia: University of Pennsylvania Press, 1970. The collected moves of the father of kinesics.

BOSMAJIAN, H. A., ed. *The Rhetoric of Nonverbal Communication*. Glenview, Ill.: Scott, Foresman, 1971. A readable collection of nonempirical essays.

DARWIN, CHARLES. *The Expression of Emotions in Man and Animals*. London: John Murray, 1872. Republished. Chicago: University of Chicago Press, 1965. A classic classic.

DAVIS, MARTHA. *Understanding Body Movement: An Annotated Bibliography*. New York: Arno Press, 1972. A well-annotated bib. of 931 items.

DUNCAN, STARKEY, JR. "Nonverbal Communication," *Psychological Bulletin*, 72, 1969, 118–37. A summary of empirical research.

EFRON, DAVID. *Gesture and Environment*. New York: King's Crown, 1941. Republished in a new edition entitled *Gesture, Race, and Culture*. The Hague: Mouton, 1972.

EISENBERG, ABNE M., and RALPH R. SMITH. *Nonverbal Communication*. Indianapolis: Bobbs-Merrill, 1971. Introductory, readable.

EKMAN, PAUL. "Universals and Cultural Differences in Facial Expressions of Emotion." In *Nebraska Symposium on Motivation, 1971*, edited by

JAMES COLE. Lincoln: University of Nebraska Press, 1972. Lays out the arguments and evidence for panhuman facial affect displays.

EKMAN, PAUL, ed. *Darwin and Facial Expression.* New York: Academic Press, 1973. A look at Darwin's century of impact.

EKMAN, PAUL, and WALLACE V. FRIESEN. "The Repertoire of Nonverbal Behavior: Categories, Origins, Usage, and Coding," *Semiotica,* 1, 1969, 49–98. A key theoretic work.

EKMAN, PAUL; WALLACE V. FRIESEN; and PHOEBE ELLSWORTH. *Emotion in the Human Face: Guidelines for Research and an Integration of Findings.* New York: Pergamon, 1972. A definitive critique of research on the face.

FAST, JULIUS. *Body Language.* New York: M. Evans, 1970. Popular; draws heavily on kinesic research.

FRANK, LAWRENCE K. "Tactile Communication," *Genetic Psychology Monographs,* 56, 1957, 209–55. A classic work on touch.

FRINGS, HUBERT and MABEL. *Animal Communication.* Waltham, Mass.: Blaisdell Publishing, 1964. A readable introduction to animal interaction.

GOFFMAN, ERVING. *The Presentation of Self in Everyday Life.* Garden City, N.Y.: Doubleday, 1959. Goffman's first and one of his best.

———. *Behavior in Public Places.* New York: Free Press, 1963. Anecdotal and insightful.

———. *Relations in Public.* New York: Basic Books, 1971. His eighth book; all of them touch on nonverbal behavior.

HALL, EDWARD T. *The Silent Language.* New York: Doubleday, 1959. Explorations in time and space.

———. *The Hidden Dimension.* Garden City, N.Y.: Doubleday, 1966. Hall back, deep in space.

HARRISON, RANDALL. "Nonverbal Communication." In *Handbook of Communication,* edited by ITHIEL DE SOLA POOL, WILBUR SCHRAMM, NATHAN MACCOBY, FRED FRY, EDWIN B. PARKER, and L. FEIN. Chicago: Rand-McNally, 1973. A review of the empirical research.

HINDE, ROBERT A. *Non-Verbal Communication.* Cambridge: Cambridge University Press, 1972. Heavy but excellent; done by a special committee of the British Royal Society.

HOWARD, JANE. *Please Touch.* New York: Dell, 1970. A pop peek at the encounter movements.

IZARD, C. E. *Face of Emotion.* New York: Appleton-Century-Crofts, 1971. Good review of research on the face.

Journal of Communication, December, 1972. A special issue devoted to nonverbal communication.

KNAPP, MARK L. *Nonverbal Communication in Human Interaction.* New York: Holt, Rinehart and Winston, 1972. Readable; good review of literature.

McLUHAN, MARSHALL. *Understanding Media.* New York: McGraw-Hill, 1964. Well, if you haven't read something of McLuhan's you probably should.

Mehrabian, Albert. *Silent Messages*. Belmont, Calif.: Wadsworth, 1971. Short popular version of Mehrabian's approach.

————. *Nonverbal Communication*. Chicago: Aldine-Atherton, 1972. A fuller treatment and wrapup of the literature.

Meyer, Leonard B. *Emotion and Meaning in Music*. Chicago: University of Chicago Press, 1956. One view of how music communicates emotion.

Montagu, Ashley. *Touching: The Human Significance of Skin*. New York: Columbia University Press, 1971. In-depth look at the importance of touch.

Nierenberg, Gerard I., and Henry H. Calero. *How To Read A Person Like A Book*. New York: Hawthorn, 1971. Popularized; from an expert on negotiating.

Poiret, Maude. *Body Talk*. New York: Universal Publishing and Distributing Corp., 1971. Popular, oversimple, but readable.

Ruesch, Jurgen, and Weldon Kees. *Nonverbal Communication: Notes on the Visual Perception of Human Relations*. Berkeley: University of California Press, 1956. Second edition, 1971. A pioneer; still worth a look.

Scheflen, Albert E. *Body Language and The Social Order*. Englewood Cliffs, N.J.: Prentice-Hall, 1972. A key work by a major researcher in kinesics.

Schutz, William. *Joy*. New York: Grove Press, 1967. Encountering a pioneer of encountering.

Sebeok, Thomas A., ed. *Animal Communication*. Bloomington: Indiana University Press, 1968. A thick compendium of animal literature.

Sebeok, Thomas A.; Alfred S. Hayes; and Mary C. Bateson, eds. *Approaches to Semiotics*. The Hague: Mouton, 1964. A major conference on paralanguage and kinesics.

Sommer, Robert. *Personal Space*. Englewood Cliffs, N.J.: Prentice-Hall, 1969. An examination of the use of space.

————. *Design Awareness*. San Francisco: Holt, Rinehart, 1972. A look at the problems of designing public space.

Tomkins, Silvan S. *Affect, Imagery, Consciousness*. New York: Springer, Vol. 1, 1962, Vol. 2, 1963. Basic theoretic work on emotion and the face.

Watzlawick, Paul; Janet H. Beavin; and Don D. Jackson. *Pragmatics of Human Communication*. New York: W. W. Norton, 1967. Moves interestingly from therapy to implications in everyday communication.

Watson, O. Michael. *Proxemic Behavior: A Cross-Cultural Study*. The Hague: Mouton, 1970. An empirical investigation of the use of space.

Wiener, Morton; Shannon Devoe; Stuart Rubinow; and Jesse Geller. "Nonverbal Behavior and Nonverbal Communication," *Psychological Review*, 79, 1972, 185–214. A proposal for one theoretic formulation and resulting research.

A

answers to "right-right"

On the basis of available clues, the best guesses for the "Right"–"Right" questions are as follows:

1	a.	T	5	a.	4	9	a.	2
	b.	F		b.	5		b.	4
	c.	5		c.	3		c.	3
2	a.	F	6	a.	1		d.	4
	b.	F		b.	5		e.	5
	c.	4		c.	F			
3	a.	4	7	a.	4			
	b.	4		b.	3			
	c.	F		c.	5			
	d.	F	8	a.	2			
4	a.	3		b.	F			
	b.	4		c.	F			
	c.	F		d.	4			

As the picture is progressively revealed, some of these early inferences prove to be "wrong." Strictly by chance, you should have been able to guess five true–false and four multiple-choice questions. Most people, however, do better than nine right. Whatever your score, the important observation is: you made a complex set of inferences on the basis of very simple nonverbal cues—and possibly without much awareness.

information-processing test

NOTE: Do *not* read the material that is printed upside down on this page. To take the test, give this book to another person and have him follow the instructions for administering the test to you. The test is discussed in Chapter 7.

The purpose of this test is to determine which way a person looks (left or right) when he is thinking about how to answer a question. To give the test sit directly facing the other person, across a table or just in an open space in a room.

Ask the following questions while the other person is looking at you. When you have finished a question the other person will look away as he thinks about how to answer. Take careful note of the direction of his very first eye movement when he looks away. Record whether that first movement was to his right or to his left.

If something goes wrong on any of the questions, make up a similar question and try again. For instance, the other person might not be looking at you as you ask the question, or he might not look away before he answers.

Here are five questions to use.

	R	L
1. How many letters are there in the word "anthropology"?	—	—
2. Tell me an English word that begins with L and ends with C.	—	
3. If you were elected President, what would be your first act to help solve the racial problems of this country?	—	
4. How many letters are there in the word "Washington"?	—	—
5. With your eyes open try to have an image of a person crying.	—	—

If the other person looked to his right more often than to his left, he is a "right looker." If he looked to his left more often, he is a "left looker."

who touches whom, where

The chart shows the data gathered by Sidney Jourard on a group of U.S. college students. Most students, men and women, reported hand contact with both mother and father and best friends of the same and opposite sex. Beyond that, however, sharp differences exist in who touches whom where. (See illustration, Fig. 8–3, p. 142.)

On:	MALES TOUCHED BY:				FEMALES TOUCHED BY:			
	Mother	Father	Girl Friend	Boy Friend	Mother	Father	Boy Friend	Girl Friend
1. Top of head	Many	Some	Some	Most	Most	Many	Many	Most
2. Face	Many	Some	Few	Most	Many	Many	Some	Most
3. Neck	Many	Some	Some	Most	Many	Many	Some	Most
4. Shoulders	Many	Some	Many	Most	Many	Many	Some	Most
5. Upper arm	Many	Many	Many	Most	Most	Many	Many	Most
6. Lower arm	Many	Many	Many	Most	Most	Many	Most	Most
7. Hand	Most	Most	Most	Most	Most	Most	Most	Most
8. Chest	Some	Few	Some	Most	Few	Few	Few	Many
9. Stomach	Some	Few	Some	Most	Few	Few	Few	Many
10. Pelvic area	Few	Few	Few	Many	Few	Few	Few	Some
11. Upper leg	Few	Few	Some	Many	Few	Few	Few	Many
12. Knee	Few	Few	Some	Many	Many	Few	Few	Most
13. Lower leg	Some	Few	Some	Many	Many	Few	Few	Many
14. Foot	Some	Few	Some	Many	Many	Few	Some	Many

The terms Few, Some, Many, and Most reflect ranges of percentages: Few, 0–25% reported such contact; Some, 26–50%; Many, 51–75%; and Most, 76–100%.

a glossary of key terms

The following terms are a few of the concepts used by researchers of nonverbal communication. The definitions given are brief, introductory orientations; frequently the concept is more complex than a few words would suggest. Similarly, the same term may be used by different authors to denote different phenomena. Where a term was introduced into the literature by a particular author, his name appears in parentheses.

ABSTRACTION. An analogic symbol that captures feeling, function, or connotation; compare *icon* and *schematic*.

ACTION LANGUAGE. Movement not done with the intent to communicate but which is informative; compare *sign language, object language* (Ruesch & Kees).

ADAPTORS. Behaviors originating in the adaptation of the individual to his environment. Three types: behaviors directed toward self, object, or alter; compare *illustrators, emblems, regulators, affect displays* (Ekman & Friesen).

AFFECT DISPLAYS. Nonverbal behavior, such as facial expressions, that reflect emotional states; compare *adaptors, emblems, illustrators, regulators* (Ekman & Friesen).

ALLOKINE. One of a number of nondistinctive variants of a *kineme* or gestural unit.

ANALOGIC. A relationship between sign and referent in which aspects of the referent are preserved in the sign; compare *digital*.

ARTIFACTUAL CODES. Sign sets arising from the use of objects; compare *performance, spatio-temporal, mediatory codes*.

BANDS. The channels and sensory receptors available for transmitting and receiving either verbal or nonverbal signs.

BATON. A type of *illustrator* (gesture) that provides emphasis, accent, punctuation.

BLEND. An *affect display* that combines emotional cues, e.g., a surprised, raised brow with a happy, smiling mouth.

CADEME. A basic element in film communication; a shot as it comes from the camera; see *edeme, vidistics* (Worth).

CODE. A set of transformations; a cluster of *markers* with rules for organization and interpretation; see *artifactual, mediatory, performance, spatio-temporal codes.*

COMMUNICATIVE. Done with intent to communicate; compare *informative, interactive* (Ekman & Friesen).

CUE. A stimulus that elicits response from some organism.

DIGITAL. A relationship between sign and referent in which the signs are discrete and arbitrary, e.g., letters and numbers; compare *analogic.*

DISPLAY RULE. A rule that modifies the display of nonverbal behavior such as affect cues; may intensify, deintensify, neutralize, or mask.

EDEME. A basic unit in film communication; the edited film shot; see *cademe, vidistics,* Fig. 4-3 (Worth).

EMBLEM. A highly stylized nonverbal behavior with well-articulated meaning; compare *adaptors, affect displays, illustrators, regulators* (Ekman & Friesen).

GLYPTICS. The study of written, verbal symbols; Fig. 4-3.

ICON. An analogic symbol that, in particular, preserves outward appearance of the referent; compare *abstraction, schematic.*

ICONICITY. The degree to which a sign or sign pattern resembles its referent.

IDEOGRAPHS. *Illustrators* (gestures) that trace the flow of a thought or idea.

ILLUSTRATORS. Nonverbal behaviors that accompany speech, elaborating, punctuating, commenting upon. Term includes: *batons, ideographs, kinetographs, pictographs, pointers, spatials;* compare *adaptors, affect displays, emblems, regulators* (Ekman & Friesen).

INFORMATIVE. Not necessarily done with intent to communicate, but interpretable by an observer; compare *communicative, interactive* (Ekman & Friesen).

INTERACTIVE. Describes nonverbal behavior that may not be done with intent to communicate and may be responded to with little awareness but yet has an observable effect on interaction; compare *communicative, informative* (Ekman & Friesen).

KINE. A rudimentary unit of movement in *kinesics*; see Fig. 4-3 (Birdwhistell).

KINEME. A unit of body movement comparable to the *phoneme* in linguistics; see *kinesics* (Birdwhistell).

KINEMORPH. A unit of body movement made up of one or more *kinemes*; see *kinesics*, Fig. 4-3 (Birdwhistell).

KINESICS. The system and study of body movement in communication; see Fig. 4-3 (Birdwhistell).

KINETOGRAPH. An *illustrator* (gesture) that demonstrates or reenacts some bodily action (Ekman & Friesen).

MARKER. A stimulus transmitted between two components of a system, i.e., a sign-vehicle. Differently in *kinesics*: a movement that marks off speech or interaction.

MEDIATORY CODES. Sign sets arising in the use of media such as film, art, music; examples include cuts, fades, cropping.

MESSAGE-SPACE. The space taken up by a message; may be the same as, less than, or more than "event-space."

MESSAGE-TIME. The time it takes to decode or process a message; may be the same as, less than, or more than "event-time."

MICROFACIALS. Fleeting facial expressions, sometimes difficult to detect with the naked eye.

MORPHEME. In linguistics, a minimum distinctive unit of grammar, e.g., a word is composed of one or more morphemes.

NONVERBAL COMMUNICATION. As used in this text: the exchange of information through nonlinguistic signs.

OBJECT LANGUAGE. The use and display of material items, both intentional and unintentional; compare *sign language* and *action language* (Ruesch & Kees).

PARALANGUAGE. The system of "extra verbal" elements that accompany speech, including voice quality, vocal qualifiers, and vocal segregates.

PARTIALS. Affect displays involving only part of the face, e.g., a surprised, raised brow but neutral eyes and mouth.

PERFORMANCE CODES. Sign sets produced with the human body, e.g., facial expressions, hand gestures, body movements; compare *artifactual, mediatory* and *spatio-temporal codes.*

PHONE. In linguistics, a rudimentary vocal sound.

PHONEME. In linguistics, a basic sound unit; a *morpheme* is composed of one or more phonemes; see Fig. 4-3.

PICT. A rudimentary unit in drawing; the counterpart of a *phone* in speech.

PICTEME. The basic unit in a pictorial code; the counterpart of a *phoneme* in speech.

PICTICS. The system and study of pictorial communication, especially drawing.

PICTOGRAPH. An *illustrator* (gesture) that draws a picture or shape in the air (Ekman & Friesen).

PICTOMORPH. The minimum distinctive pictorial unit; parallel to the morph or *morpheme* level in speech; see Fig. 4-3.

POINTERS. *Illustrators* (gestures) that point to a referent; also called "deictic" movements.

POINTS. Movements, e.g., of eye or head, that punctuate the structural flow of interaction; compare *positions, presentations* (Scheflen).

POSITIONS. Larger divisions of interaction, incorporating one or more *points;* compare *presentation* (Scheflen).

PRESENTATIONS. Major divisions of interaction, incorporating one or more *positions;* compare *points, positions* (Scheflen).

PROXEMICS. The system and study of behavioral patterns associated with the use of space; see Fig. 4-3 (Hall).

REGULATORS. A type of body movement, such as head-nods, that regulates the flow of interaction; compare *adaptors, affect displays, emblems, illustrators* (Ekman & Friesen).

SCHEMATIC. An analogic sign that captures relationships or structure of the referent, e.g., maps, blueprints, diagrams; compare *icon, abstraction.*

SEQUENTIAL SYNTAX. The organization of code elements sequentially in time or space, e.g., most verbal sign patterns; compare *synchronic syntax.*

SIGN. A stimulus (marker) that "stands for" some other event for some interpreter; compare *signal, symbols.*

SIGN LANGUAGE. The purposeful use of gestures to replace words; compare *action language* and *object language* (Ruesch & Kees).

SIGN PATTERN. A configuration of signs; a system of sign elements.

SIGNAL. One type of *sign;* it is likely to "announce" another sign or to elicit an action response; compare *symbol.*

SPATIALS. *Illustrators* (gestures) that indicate size or relationship.

SPATIO-TEMPORAL CODES. Sign sets emerging in the use of time and space; compare *artifactual, mediatory, performance codes.*

SYMBOL. A type of *sign,* emphasizing denotative and connotative meaning; compare *signal.*

SYNCHRONIC SYNTAX. The organization of code elements, simultaneously in time or space, e.g., picture layout; compare *sequential syntax.*

SYSTEM. A set of interrelated elements; the system is separated from its environment by a boundary; several levels may be present: suprasystem, system, subsystem, and component.

VIDISTICS. The system and study of cinematic communication; see Fig. 4-3 (Worth).

index

Timing, 113, 123
Tomkins, Silvan S., 119, 203
Tone, 72
Touch, 142, 195
Truman, Harry S., 171
Typography, 104

Uncertainty, 25, 64–65, 99

"V"-gesture, 138
Verbal:
  contribution, 109
  difference from nonverbal, 72–73
  mediators, 82
Verbalizers, 85 (see also Brain)

Vidistics, 72, 200
Visualizers, 85 (see also Brain)
Vocal characterizers, 97, 108, 112
Vocal qualifiers, 97, 107, 108, 112
  extent (see Extent, vocal)
  intensity (see Intensity, vocal)
  pitch (see Pitch)
Vocal segregates, 97, 108–9, 112

Watson, Michael O., 72, 126, 203
Watzlawick, Paul, 31, 203
White, Benjamin W., 143
White, Theodore H., 173
Wiener, Morton, 136, 203
Worth, Sol, 197
Wright, Frank Lloyd, 147